P9-DEV-299

BY GITA MEHTA

KARMA COLA

RAJ

A RIVER SUTRA

A RIVER SUTRA

NAN A. TALESE

DOUBLEDAY

NEW YORK

LONDON

TORONTO

SYDNEY

AUCKLAND

GITA MEHTA

A

RIVER

SUTRA

PUBLISHED BY NAN A. TALESE
an imprint of Doubleday, a division of
Bantam Doubleday Dell Publishing Group, Inc.
1540 Broadway, New York, New York 10036

DOUBLEDAY and the portrayal of an anchor
with a dolphin are trademarks of
Doubleday, a division of Bantam Doubleday Dell
Publishing Group, Inc.

All of the characters in this book are fictitious,
and any resemblance to actual persons, living or
dead, is purely coincidental.

Book design by Marysarah Quinn

Library of Congress Cataloging-in-Publication Data
Mehta, Gita.
A river Sutra / Gita Mehta. — 1st ed.
p.   cm.
1. Pilgrims and pilgrimages—India—Fiction.   2. Tales—India.
I. Title.
PS3563.E344R58   1993
813′.54—dc20   92-35779
                                                  CIP

ISBN 0-385-47007-X

Copyright © 1993 by Gita Mehta

All Rights Reserved
Printed in the United States of America
June 1993

1 3 5 7 9 10 8 6 4 2

FIRST EDITION

FOR ADITYA

Listen, O brother.

Man is the greatest truth.

Nothing beyond.

LOVE SONGS OF CHANDIDAS

CHAPTER ONE

The Government still pays my wages but I no longer think of myself as a bureaucrat. Bureaucrats belong too much to the world, and I have fulfilled my worldly obligations. I am now a vanaprasthi, someone who has retired to the forest to reflect.

Of course, I was forced to modify tradition, having spent my childhood in Bombay and my career as a civil servant working only in cities. Although my desire to withdraw from the world grew more urgent as I aged, I knew I was simply not equipped to wander into the jungle and become a forest hermit, surviving on fruit and roots.

Then shortly after my wife passed away I

learned of a vacant post at a Government rest house situated on the Narmada River. I had often stayed in such rest houses while touring the countryside on official business. Over time I had even developed an affection for these lonely sanctuaries built by the Moghul emperors across the great expanse of India to shelter the traveler and the pilgrim, a practice wisely maintained by subsequent administrations.

But the bungalow's proximity to the Narmada River was its particular attraction. The river is among our holiest pilgrimage sites, worshipped as the daughter of the god Shiva. During a tour of the area I had been further intrigued to discover the criminal offense of attempted suicide is often ignored if the offender is trying to kill himself in the waters of the Narmada.

To the great surprise of my colleagues, I applied for the humble position of manager of the Narmada rest house. At first they tried to dissuade me, convinced that grief over my wife's death had led to my aberrant request. Senior bureaucrats, they argued, should apply for higher office. Finding me adamant, they finally recommended me for the post and then forgot me.

For several years now, thanks to the recommendations of my former colleagues, this rest house situated halfway up a hill of the Vindhya Range has been my forest retreat.

It is a double-storeyed building constructed from copper-colored local stone, the upper floor comprising three spacious and self-contained suites which overlook the gardens, the ground floor occupied by a dining room and drawing room opening onto a wide veranda. Happily, the interiors retain their original mosaic tiles, having escaped the attentions of a British administrator who plastered the outside walls at the turn of the century, giving the exterior of the bungalow with its pillared portico and balustraded steps an air more Victorian than Moghul.

To one side of the gardens, hidden by mango trees, is a small cottage in which I live. On the other side, the gardens lead to a stone terrace overlooking the Narmada, which flows seven hundred feet below.

Spanning a mile from bank to bank, the river has become the object of my reflections.

A great aid to my meditations is the beauty of our location. Across the sweep of water, I can see fertile fields stretching for miles and miles into the southern horizon until they meet the gray shadows of the Satpura Hills. On this riverbank towering bamboo thickets and trees overgrown with wild jasmine and lantana creepers cover the hill-sides, suspending the bungalow in jungle so dense I cannot see the town of Rudra, only nineteen kilometers away, where my clerk, Mr. Chagla, lives.

Poor Mr. Chagla must bicycle for over an hour to reach us, but as we are without a telephone his daily return to town is vital for organizing our supplies and attending to other business. Rudra has the nearest post office, as well as a doctor who presides over a small hospital and a branch police station with four constables.

Below Rudra, visible from our terrace at the bend of the river, sprawls the temple complex of Mahadeo. At sunset I often sit on the terrace with our bungalow guests to watch the distant figures of the pilgrims silhouetted against the brilliant crimsons of the evening sky descending the stone steps that lead from Mahadeo's many temples to the river's edge. With twilight, the water at Mahadeo starts flickering with tiny flames as if catching fire from the hundreds of clay lamps being floated downstream for the evening devotions.

My day usually begins on this terrace. I have formed the habit of rising before dawn to sit here in the dark with my face turned toward the river's source, an underground spring that surfaces four hundred kilometers to the east.

In the silence of the ebbing night I sometimes

think I can hear the river's heartbeat pulsing under the ground before she reveals herself at last to the anchorites of Shiva deep in meditation around the holy tank at Amarkantak. I imagine the ascetics sitting in the darkness like myself, their naked bodies smeared in ash, their matted hair wound on top of their heads in imitation of their Ascetic god, witnessing the river's birth as they chant:

"Shiva-o-ham, Shiva-o-ham,
I that am Shiva, Shiva am I."

Then streaks of pale light send clouds of noisy birds into the sky, evoking crowds of pilgrims swarming through Amarkantak's temples for the morning worship.

By the time the red ball of the sun appears over the hills, the activity I have been imagining at the river's source becomes the reality of the rest house with the appearance of our gardeners, our sweepers, and the milkman.

After issuing instructions to the early staff, I leave the bungalow by the northern gate for my morning walk. Almost immediately I enter the jungle. Under the great trees glistening with dew —teak, peepul, silk cotton, mango, banyan—the mud path is still deserted, crossed only by bounding monkeys, leaping black buck, meandering wild boar as if the animals are glorying in their brief possession of the jungle. On my return in two hours I will be greeted on this path by sturdy tribal women from the nearby village of Vano collecting fuel for their cooking fires.

Our bungalow guards are hired from Vano village and enjoy a reputation for fierceness as descendants of the tribal races that held the Aryan invasion of India at bay for centuries in these hills. Indeed, the Vano village deity is a stone image of a half-woman with the full breasts of a fertility symbol but the torso of a coiled snake, because the tribals believe they once ruled a great snake kingdom until they were defeated by the gods of the Aryans. Saved from annihilation only by a divine personification of the Narmada River, the grateful tribals conferred on the river the gift of annulling the effects of snakebite, and I have often heard pilgrims who have never met a tribal reciting the invocation

Salutation in the morning and at night to
    thee, O Narmada!
Defend me from the serpent's poison.

The Vano villagers also believe their goddess cures madness, liberating those who are possessed.

Beyond the valley on the next range of hills is a Muslim village with a small mosque adjoining the tomb of Amir Rumi, a Sufi saint of the sixteenth century. My friend Tariq Mia is mullah of the village mosque, and most mornings I walk all the way to the village in order to chat with Tariq Mia, for the old man is the wisest of all my friends.

On my way to Tariq Mia I sometimes pause at the summit of our hill to enjoy the view. Between the eastern hills I can see foaming waterfalls where the river plummets through marble canyons into the valley below the rest house, and if I turn west I can watch the river broadening as it races toward the Arabian Sea to become seventeen kilometers wide at its delta.

A day seldom passes when I do not see white-robed pilgrims walking on the riverbanks far below me. Many are like myself, quite elderly persons who have completed the first stages of life prescribed by our Hindu scriptures—the infant, the student, the householder—and who have now entered the stage of the vanaprasthi, to seek personal enlightenment.

I am always astonished at their endurance, since I know the Narmada pilgrimage to be an arduous affair that takes nearly two years to complete. At the mouth of the river on the Arabian Sea, the pilgrims must don white clothing out of respect for Shiva's asceticism before walking eight hundred kilometers to the river's source at Amarkantak. There they must cross to the opposite bank of the river and walk all the way back to the ocean, pausing only during the monsoon rains in some small temple town like Mahadeo, which has accommodated the legions of devout who have walked this route millennium upon millennium.

Then I remind myself that the purpose of the pilgrimage is endurance. Through their endurance the pilgrims hope to generate the heat, the tapas, that links men to the energy of the universe, as the Narmada River is thought to link mankind to the energy of Shiva.

It is said that Shiva, Creator and Destroyer of Worlds, was in an ascetic trance so strenuous that rivulets of perspiration began flowing from his body down the hills. The stream took on the form of a woman—the most dangerous of her kind: a beautiful virgin innocently tempting even ascetics to pursue her, inflaming their lust by appearing at one moment as a lightly dancing girl, at another as a romantic dreamer, at yet another as a seductress loose-limbed with the lassitude of desire. Her inventive variations so amused Shiva that he named her Narmada, the Delightful One, blessing her with the words "You shall be forever holy, forever inexhaustible." Then he gave her in marriage to the ocean, Lord of Rivers, most lustrous of all her suitors.

Standing here on the escarpment of the hill, a light wind cooling my body after its exertions, I can see the river flowing to meet her bridegroom in all those variations that delighted the Ascetic while on her banks the pilgrims move slowly toward their destination. From this distance the white-robed men and women seem the spume of the river's waves, and as I watch them I wait to hear the sound of Tariq Mia's voice calling the faithful to prayer.

I do not wish to arrive before the old mullah has completed his priestly duties, so if I am early and have not yet heard the sound of "Allah-ho-Akbar!" echoing in the valley that separates us, I walk to a row of ancient Jain caves cut into the copper stone.

I never enter the caves, for fear of snakes, unable to believe that even the Narmada will protect me from a serpent's fangs. Instead I sit on a large boulder at one side peering into their darkness. The caves have been deserted for centuries, but I am always hopeful of encountering some passing Jain traveler who may have stopped here for a moment's worship.

Once I met two naked Jain mendicants, members of the Sky Clad sect whose rigorous penances include the denial of human shame. To my great disappointment they indicated by signs that they no longer even spoke. After smiling at them for half an hour I regretfully took my leave.

On another occasion I met a Jain monk from another sect who had only recently renounced the world.

I remember the encounter well. It was winter and I was sitting on my boulder, the winter sun warming my face. In my hands was a bunch of bananas I had broken off a tree during my walk as a gift for Tariq Mia. I was about to peel one for myself when someone coughed behind me.

I turned to see a slender figure robed in white muslin standing at my side. Under his shaved head, his large eyes examined me with peculiar intensity. A muslin mask covered his mouth but I could hear him clearly when he asked, "If I continue on this road will I reach Mahadeo?"

I explained the route to Mahadeo, curiosity compelling me to find some way of delaying him in conversation. Then I saw the begging bowl in his hand. "May I offer you some fruit?"

He accepted and I placed the bananas in his bowl. "Are you making the Narmada pilgrimage?"

"I am not of the Hindu faith. I am joining my fellow Jain monks in Mahadeo, where they have gone to find a barber. We will beg him to do us the charity of shaving our heads."

I pretended ignorance to keep him talking. "Why must you shave your heads?"

"To avoid human vanity."

"Do you cover your mouths for the same reason?"

"No. These masks prevent us from killing some blameless insect by sudden inhalation." He removed his mask in order to eat, revealing the strong lines of a handsome face only slightly marred by a jutting chin. "A Jain monk seeks to free himself of the fetters of worldly desire through the vows of poverty, celibacy, and nonviolence."

"Tell me, friend, which of such harsh vows is the most difficult for a man to keep?"

He smiled, and the sudden relaxation of his austere expression showed him to be a young man, not more than thirty years of age. "This may surprise you. Nonviolence. It is very tiring to be worrying all the time that you may be harming some living thing. I must always look down while walking for fear that I may step on an ant. Even plucking bananas becomes an act fraught with danger. Who knows what small creatures live in the leaves or trunk of a banana tree?"

1 1

He fell silent and I watched him surreptitiously as he ate. When he had finished he folded the banana skins and placed them neatly at the base of the boulder. As he retied the mask over his mouth I remarked with some diffidence, "I have also renounced the world."

"Was there a great ceremony to mark the moment of your departure?"

I nearly laughed, remembering the views of my colleagues, but I only said, "My wife was barren so I had no children to concern themselves with my decision. My parents are no longer alive, nor my wife, and my associates hardly noticed the moment of my departure."

"You are fortunate. My father boasts of spending sixty-two million rupees on my renunciation ceremonies."

"Did you say sixty-two rupees?" I thought I must have misheard him through the mask.

"No. Sixty-two million rupees."

"Million! *Sixty-two* million! How is such a thing possible? Please explain your ceremony to me."

"It is not appropriate for me to discuss the life I forfeited when I became a monk."

I persisted. "It is your duty to enlighten me. You are still a young man. I have much to learn from someone who gave up the world so early—"

"Do not put such value on my actions," the monk interrupted me sternly. "Giving up the world was no sacrifice for me."

"But what a sacrifice for your father! Sixty-two million rupees!"

I patted the boulder, inviting him to sit by me. "We Hindus revere the spiritual teachings contained in our Upanishads. Do you know what the word upanishad means? It means to sit beside and listen. Here I am, sitting, eager to listen. As a monk, can you deny me enlightenment?"

He flung his head back, blowing the thin muslin of his mask outward with the force of his uninhibited laughter. "You Hindus. Always disguising your greed with your many-headed gods and your many-headed arguments."

He placed his begging bowl at the foot of the boulder. "But if my story will help you on the path of truth, you are welcome to it."

Walking to a nearby tree, he retrieved a wooden stick tied with tufts of wool. For several minutes he carefully brushed the boulder free of insects. Satisfied at last that he would be harming no living creature, to my delight he climbed up beside me.

CHAPTER TWO

THE MONK'S STORY

I have loved just one thing in my life.

You ask about the ritual with which I gained the freedom to pursue this love. Why? Ritual means nothing if you do not know the longing that precedes it.

Can the love between a man and woman be contained in the flowers they exchange, or a coin contain a merchant's love of wealth? But if you must have only the symbols of love, not love itself, imagine it then.

I am standing in the suffocating heat of a sports stadium, watching the hysteria of forty thousand people. Each time I move there is a roar of approval, as if in just breathing I am doing something extraordinary.

Garlands of diamonds circle my neck, winking in the brilliant morning sunshine. Winking, did I say? Flashing. Filling the stadium with galaxies of light.

On my head is a turban. Tied to it are strings of solitaire diamonds that hang down over my face, hiding me from the appetite of the crowds screaming my name. But it is not only the diamonds that are exciting the crowds. It is also, and more acutely so, their disbelief that I am giving up my wealth.

Everyone in the stadium knows I am heir to an empire that stretches from the diamond mines of Africa and the diamond cutters of India to the diamond auctions of Hong Kong, Tel Aviv, Moscow; the trading houses of Antwerp; the banking establishments of Zurich. My father owns one of the largest diamond companies in the world, and today's procession is only the culmination of a dozen ceremonies already held all over the world when limousines filled with members of the international diamond trading community followed the Rolls-Royce in which I rode beside my father to distribute our charity at the offices of the Red Cross and UNICEF.

I can feel the angry skepticism in the stadium even before I hear the yelled jeers below the podium on which I am standing with my father.

"Arrey, Ashok bhai. O brother Ashok, how will you live without your luxuries?"

"No Rolls-Royce and driver to bring you home when you tire of your spiritual game, brother. Think again while you still have time."

A row of young men with brilliantined hair are laughing below me. When they see me inclining toward them, they clasp hands and jump in the air.

"Poor Ashok! No more whisky, no more cards!"

"No more airplanes to take you to Gay Pareeee!"

"Remember, brother. You will never be able to lie between the thighs of a woman again."

"Oh, Ashok, repent your vanity! It is not human to give up those silken caresses."

"Those long black tresses!"

Their betel-stained mouths open in raucous laughter and they slap each other's shoulders in glee. How can these jeering youths understand how keenly I have waited to be free of the world? They sit in cheap cinema halls staring in hopeless longing at some voluptuous screen siren whereas I have possessed those female icons in such surfeit that I have sickened of them.

A group of musicians climbs onto the podium. For a moment my view is obscured by a trombone. All I can see is dust being kicked up from the playing fields, which have become powdery with summer drought. The temperature is over 110 degrees. Under the intense sun my head begins to swim, but if I ask for water I know it will be lukewarm.

There is no ice left in the city. No bottled soft drinks, no vegetables, no fruit. Yesterday my father fed twenty thousand people in this stadium, and lorries are bringing supplies from Ahmedabad City, sixty miles away, to feed another twenty thousand here tomorrow.

In any case I cannot ask for water. I have begun my fast. This morning I took my last meal with my family although I was not hungry, unable to ignore the tears falling from my wife's eyes onto the table as she silently placed my favorite dishes before me. I am forbidden further sustenance until my diksha ceremony, when I finally become a monk. Only then will I be permitted to walk the streets of the city, begging my food and drink.

The thought that I must wait twenty-four hours to quench my thirst alarms me, and I fear I might faint before the procession begins, but the musicians move away from the podium, allowing me to breathe again.

A line of seven elephants lumbers past the podium. Imagine my mortification. Scenes from my life are painted in bright colors on their wrinkled skins—myself on the steps of my father's bank in Zurich, at my wedding, holding my first child.

Beside me my father glows with pride. He telephoned a friend who owns one of the big Bombay film studios, and the movie moghul responded by sending him a dozen poster painters whose garish art already deforms the city with billboards of forthcoming attractions. Today, displayed in all its stunning vulgarity on the buttocks, the haunches, the legs, the waving trunks, even the flapping ears of elephants, is the fruit of their most recent labors—my life.

One beast ignores the imprecations of the elephant keeper, backing toward the podium, and I face a portrait of myself dressed as a cricket player throwing a cricket ball at a row of wickets painted on the elephant's other leg. The mahout succeeds in urging the elephant forward. The wickets bend like rubber each time the elephant takes a step.

Loud cheers sweep across the stadium. A cavalcade of horses is trotting toward me. Gold cloths cover the saddles under the riders, golden tassels sweep the dust. The riders spur their horses into a canter around the field and the crowds push back into the benches, yelling their appreciation until their attention is diverted by the camels swaying through the stadium gates, pulling camel carts crowded with musicians, veiled singing women, men with oblong drums strapped to their shoulders.

"Eighteen, nineteen, twenty, twenty-one . . ." the crowd shouts. The drummers pound their drums in response, feeding the crowd's delirium with increasing crescendoes until all forty camel carts have rolled into the stadium.

The crowds have become accustomed to witnessing new spectacles. To their delight, hordes of dancers now whirl into the stadium, brightly lacquered sticks held aloft in their hands as they dance in widening circles before the horses. Under our podium the mahouts are herding their elephants between the ropes tied from the tusks of the first elephant to the silver-plated chariot in which I will ride beside my father. Lashed to each elephant are massive drums, traditionally used to transport oil and grain. Today those drums are filled with cash and coins to be thrown as charity to the crowds. The elephants sink to their knees and once again the crowds cheer while my younger brother, three uncles, three cousins, gingerly climb onto separate elephants, trying to look regal on their shifting perches.

· · ·

What is the purpose of this display? you ask.

Imitation, is my answer.

My father is duplicating the procession with which Mahavira, the great teacher of the Jain faith, renounced the world.

Unlike your busy pantheon of Hindu gods, we Jains follow in the footsteps of a man. A great prince it is true, but still only a man who found all his wealth, power, beauty gave him no more than transitory pleasure and who yearned for a pleasure that could be sustained. Wrapped in the luxuries of a great court by day, a beautiful young wife by night, Mahavira longed for the freedom to find this state of bliss, if it existed.

And so one day he left his gilded cage in a mighty procession with dancers clearing the way for elephants, horses, camels loaded with wealth to be distributed to the poor.

Since then, whenever a Jain becomes a monk, a procession and the distribution of charity mark his departure from the world.

But my father's grief at my renunciation of the world has become a desire to have my departure rival the splendors of the farewell of Mahavira himself.

There is pandemonium below us as the procession forms. People are surging onto the field. Guards with cane sticks beat them back, fearful a panicked animal might injure someone. I can see the riders positioning their horses in front of the camels lining up in front of the elephants roped to the silver chariot. Then my father pulls at my elbow and I follow him down the steps into the silver chariot.

The dancers whirl out of the stadium, followed by prancing horses and camel carts rolling forward on their wooden wheels. At last the elephants move ponderously through the stadium gates, dragging my silver chariot into the narrow alleys of the bazaar.

A sea of people closes on the procession as we force our way through the twisting streets toward the shop where my ancestors began their business.

Once, when I was on holiday from school in England, my father took me to the shop, laughing at my grimace of disgust when I saw the open gutter running next to the dingy wooden shack.

"You have lived too long in England. You see only the squalor of these bazaars. But this is a whole world in which the secrets of wealth are whispered from one generation to another. These alleys taught your ancestors the two things vital to success—how to sense approaching danger and how to be flexible.

"When your grandfather's grandfather first arrived here he was so poor he kept his entire stock, three small diamonds, wrapped in a cotton belt tied to his stomach underneath his shirt, never showing a stone until he was certain the buyer was serious about making a purchase.

"From the doorway of his wooden shack he studied the secrets of the bazaar. He learned how its streets changed to accommodate necessity. Widening to seduce the Moghul armies that came to put them to the sword. Contracting in times of peace to such intimate dimensions a man could cross them in two paces to pursue a bargain or secure a loan. Expanding to absorb the goods pouring out of the factories of the British Empire. Shrinking for the austerities preached by Mahatma Gandhi.

"Remember, in this squalid bazaar your family learned to negotiate, manipulate, intrigue, bargain. Armed with that knowledge—in only four generations—we parlayed three small diamonds into an empire."

Today those alleys are being carpeted in my family's wealth, bank notes trampled into their melting tarmac. Through my visor of diamond solitaires I glance at my father. He is smiling with pleasure as he watches his relatives flinging fistfuls of money to the crowds. The paper currency hangs suspended in the air for a second, like confetti, before floating gently down into the forest of grasping hands.

My father hands me a silver urn. Grateful that no one can see my shame, I plunge my hands into its glittering depths and throw pearls, diamond chips, silver coins in high arcs over the shifting mass of heads.

Silver coins clink against the tin roofs of the bazaar shops, pearls roll down the broken steps that span the gutters. For a moment the glinting gems, the mirrors in the singers' veils, the golden cloths that cover the horses, this silver chariot, all render the scene weightless and unreal. Then the crowd pushes against the guards, screaming and waving at my carriage, fearful of losing such treasure.

There is a riot as the procession turns from the bazaar. People are clambering over each other's shoulders to reach the silver carriage from which fortunes are being dispersed so carelessly into the air. I can hear the riders shouting at their rearing horses, see the guards trying to clear a way through the surging crowds as the camel carts rock wildly from side to side and the drivers fight to steady the camels.

Our chariot feels as if it is coming apart under our feet. I grip my father's arm so he will not fall. He turns and I see fear in his eyes.

I know it is a fear of violence.

When I was a child my father had taught me the cardinal doctrine of the Jains.

"The most important thing in our faith is ahimsa, the practice of nonviolence. That is why we are bankers or merchants. There are so many activities we cannot undertake for fear of harming life. If we were farmers we might unknowingly kill creatures under our plows. In industry the earth is drilled for oil, iron, coal. Can you imagine how much life is extinguished by those machines?"

"Diamonds are mined from the ground," I had argued as a child.

"I have never bought a diamond mine," my father reminded me. "Even though diamond mines would have increased the wealth of the company immeasurably. But if a man believes in the doctrine of ahimsa, he must follow it to its logical end."

Growing up I came to realize my father's dignity rested on his widely acknowledged genius as a merchant and his private adherence to the principle of nonviolence, which led him to distribute much of the company's profits in charitable trusts. I admired him more than any man alive.

Before I joined university I spent a year traveling around the world with my father acquiring an understanding of the diamond trade. During that year my attitude toward him changed. I was shocked to see he was unmoved by the conditions under which the diamonds were mined, or the distressing poverty of the miners.

I had once dared to ask, "How can you worry about a dead insect more than you care about a human being?"

My father had raised his voice at my impertinence. "What about our trusts? Are they for insects? Do you know how many people are assisted by me every day who would otherwise die of neglect? Fed and clothed, their hospital bills paid, their dead cremated. We cannot solve the problems of the world. We can only help those within our reach."

For the first time I had recognized that wealth had excised my father's emotions, freeing him to examine people as if they were abstractions. His benevolence had a cold mathematics that left him unmoved and without curiosity about those he helped.

The inhuman nature of his philanthropy had frightened me. Part of me still wished to become like him. On the rare occasions when he had allowed me to conduct a minor negotiation, I had been gratified by his congratulations, and yet all through that year I had felt an undercurrent of fear that in inheriting my father's business acumen I might also inherit his inhumanity.

Now I see the fear in my father's eyes as fists smash against the sides of our silver chariot.

My father does not comprehend poverty. He does not know why people might kill each other for the chance to escape their lives with a handful of gems thrown by his son or why, at the very moment of his greatest charitable act, he has unleashed what he hates most, violence.

The elephants are becoming agitated by the riot. The elephant keepers try to control them, striking the heads of the great beasts with iron-pronged prods until blood rolls down their ears. The elephants trumpet in rage and the mobs fall back in terror of being trampled under their immense gray feet. Ahead of us the horsemen spur their mounts into a gallop, clearing the street to allow the procession to move out of the bazaar.

There is a more sedate atmosphere as we enter the main avenue of the city. Lines of policemen are patrolling the tree-shaded pavements to prevent the spectators from climbing over the steel barriers at the side of the road.

We halt briefly. One of the elephants has twisted its foot in the rope, throwing the other elephants into confusion. The mahout dismounts to free the rope, and the animal moves sideways. I suddenly see a painting of myself embracing a featureless woman.

She does not need features. It is enough for the spectators that she is haloed in clouds of blond hair. Catcalls and wolf whistles fill the air. Even the policemen are laughing. The mahout remounts the freed elephant. I watch the blond hair melting back into the panorama of my life.

My brother is enjoying the reaction of the crowds. He leans back on his elephant seat to wave at me, and I know he is remembering my father's rage when I told him I wished to renounce the world.

My brother had been present in the room as I tried to convince my father that my decision was not a passing whim.

"It is!" my father had shouted, refusing to believe me. "I should never have allowed you to live abroad. The West has destroyed your peace of mind!"

I suppose there was some truth in my father's accusations. We had a tacit understanding that he would indulge my youth with all the wealth at his disposal until I assumed the responsibilities of the family empire. Then I would revert to the traditions of the Jains, even consenting to an arranged marriage if I had not already formed an appropriate attachment.

In doing this my father was gambling my youth and his wealth against my doubts. Over the years I had often insisted that although we did not perpetrate physical cruelty ourselves, our wealth was sustained by violence. I think my father recognized that I shared his implacable nature and feared my doubts might lead me to renounce his world.

For a while it seemed my father had calculated accurately. Knowing my years of pleasure in Europe were limited, I had seized on my irresponsible life with hectic delight. Beautiful women were lured by my fast sports cars, the wealth I squandered in fashionable discotheques, and by myself —for I was thought to be handsome with my aquiline features and my slender, muscular body. Then too, the family maintained luxurious holiday homes, and I was generous with my invitations.

If the indolent starlets from the film studios of Bombay, the ambitious secretaries from the European diamond companies, the bored girls who haunted the discotheques, sometimes felt I used a little too much force in our lovemaking, they soon laughed it off when they received my lavish presents, even boasting to their friends that I suffered from an excess of virility.

Gradually my life of unremitting pleasure ceased to satisfy me, leaving me exhausted from the last indulgence while anticipating the next. At the age of twenty-six I had already become fatigued by the world, knowing that even at the moment of gratification, the seed of new desire was being sown.

When my father suggested that it was time for me to marry, I raised no objections to sharing my life with a total stranger. The prospect of ceasing to find new means to amuse myself came as a relief.

It proved easy to control my restlessness after my return to India. My wife was a gentle creature who could not discard her formality, even in our marital bed. I treated her with corresponding courtesy, seeking only to make her comfortable with our intimacies, knowing she had neither the imagination nor the appetite for pleasure. For myself, I did not miss the sexual excesses of my earlier life, and once the birth of our daughter was followed by a son, my wife became so preoccupied with her maternal duties I no longer needed to play the husband.

In truth, I did not care what happened next. My

life was like a dreamless sleep, office routine following domestic routine without a tremor.

My wife adhered to the practice of fasting twice a week, and in an idle sort of way I began to fast myself, if only because I was dismayed at the weight I was gaining with my inactive life.

Convinced he had won the battle against my doubts, my father sent me an elderly Jain monk to sustain the efficacy of my fasts by discoursing on our traditions.

The old monk's air of contentment was so beguiling I became quite attached to him although I paid no attention to his discourses.

Every morning before I left for work I listened to his soft voice behind the muslin mask that covered his mouth, as one listens to a piece of music that is neither too loud nor too soft, too fast nor too slow.

"Do not trust the tranquility of your present mood," the old priest warned me one day. "Some upheaval most certainly awaits you."

I teased him for making astrological predictions like a Hindu. He silenced me with unexpected severity.

"You think I am only an old man reading the scriptures aloud. But I can see you are suppressing something. And what is suppressed will erupt."

I was astonished. We had never spoken of personal matters. "Why do you think so?"

"I see you withdrawing from your life, your possessions. You have even ceased eating."

I started laughing. "You came to these conclusions because I think I am too fat?"

The monk ignored my sarcasm. "You have traveled the world and think you have seen everything. Perhaps you have. But you have not yet learned the secrets of the human heart."

"How can you speak of secrets, with your blameless life?"

"My life is neither blameless nor unique. I have learned this from Mahavira's teachings."

"Ah, of course, the Great Teacher. What could he possibly know about mere mortals?"

"That they long to be free. Many men die before they learn the desire for freedom lies deep within them, like a dammed river waiting to be released. But once a man has had that momentary glimpse of freedom, he needs to be instructed further."

I sneered but at the same time I found myself intrigued by the possibility that this old monk, with his limited knowledge of the world, might know some secret of the heart that could shatter the shell of numbness that enclosed me.

As if reading my mind, the monk said slyly,

"What do you lose by hearing Mahavira's description of the skepticism and nihilism that disturb a man when he finds he is not free, although he continues to perform the role that society requires of him?"

I was taken aback. "Mahavira spoke about these things?"

The monk was amused by my reaction and offered to instruct me further.

Over the months the monk's teachings continued to surprise me. He was able to predict how I would feel long before I arrived at the emotion myself, describing to me the states of my despair with greater accuracy than I seemed able to experience them. I told the monk I longed to share his knowledge.

"But I have no knowledge. I am only describing what has been observed by others wiser than myself."

I refused to believe him. I was convinced he had some unusual power and I wanted to possess it.

The monk tried to warn me against such ambition. I would not listen. I had become like my ancestor, determined to pass through each door the monk opened, as my ancestor had walked each alley of the bazaar until he learned its secrets.

. . .

Now the dancers are whirling under the lighted archway that marks the street leading to the sprawling house built by my ancestor's wealth. My father puts his arm around my shoulder. I see tears welling in his eyes. I push aside the strings of diamond solitaires, anxious to conceal my mortification at the scale on which he has orchestrated my renunciation of the world.

I turn smiling to him, but my father's grief humbles me, forcing me to understand that this massive procession, this immense display of charity are only his attempt to give away what I have denied him from giving me, his eldest son.

He pulls me into his embrace, and I am filled with remorse at my father's sorrow as I was once overwhelmed by tenderness at his anguish.

Throughout my childhood my father had told me the ability to sense approaching danger was something possessed only by the greatest merchants. As I grew older I came to realize he prided himself on being among the handful of men who had it.

Perhaps it was that instinct that led my father to dissuade me from seeing the old monk again. "His tranquility is seductive. But you have no idea what price he may have paid for it."

I had refused indignantly. "He is trying to alleviate the suffering around him. That's good enough for me."

"We do more good through our trusts every day than he will do in a lifetime of being a monk. Without our work there would be no alms to allow him to live on charity."

I had leveled my old accusations at my father. "At least he has some humanity. You only help people to display your power."

Instead of rage, for the first time fear had colored my father's reply. "You do not understand what you are saying. There is no suffering as harsh as that of the Jain monks. Our ascetics don't believe there is any purpose to endurance. They only endure increasing pain, until they no longer fear it. I do more good than them every day without undergoing their pain."

My wife was standing at the doorway listening with concern to my father's passion.

"Their ways are bleaker than you can possibly imagine. Do you know what it means to be such a monk? Do you know the levels of asceticism he must suffer?"

My father was expressing himself with such urgency I dared not interrupt him. "Do you know how that serene old monk hopes to die? Starving himself to death. He observes respect for life when all the time he is working toward the goal of denying his own life."

He stared at me, waiting for my response, but I could not speak. His anguish had melted the numbness that froze my heart. I was overcome by compassion for him, for myself, for my concerned and curious wife, for the human helplessness that linked us all.

It was my first experience of ahimsa.

In his attempt to frighten me, my father had made me realize that to prevent suffering a man must be capable of suffering, that a man who cannot suffer is not alive.

My father could not understand why I needed to be with the monk more than ever and I could not explain, for the lesson of ahimsa must be learned by the heart, not the mind.

But I knew I could never return to the anesthesia of wealth that had for so long numbed me to the suffering that could make me human.

I told the old monk of the sudden, unexpected compassion that had overwhelmed me at my father's fear. "But it lasted for such a brief time and I have not experienced it again."

"The human heart must conquer many hurdles to recapture that vision until ahimsa can become a way of life."

"I am willing to cross the hurdles."

The old monk had smiled. "Oh, my innocent young friend. Can you overcome your disgust at all the things from which your father's wealth has protected you? Can you beg in the filth of the bazaars? Can you eat what has been discarded? Until you can do these small things you will understand neither the nonviolence of ahimsa nor gain freedom from the world."

The procession has halted at our gates, and guards are steering the camel carts and mounted riders down a side street. People are running from the house to help my relatives dismount from the elephants.

As I walk past the milling dancers I can see the women of the house weeping on the balcony—my wife, my mother, my sister-in-law, my cousins. But I know they are reconciled to my departure, their tears are only an overflow from the excitement of the day.

On the veranda the children are waiting to bid me farewell. They are too young to understand what I am doing, and I do not wish to frighten them so I embrace them as I would have done on any other evening.

When I reach my chambers the servants help me undress, freeing me of the diamond helmet and the garlands of gems that have suffocated me all day. I enter the silence of my marble bathroom. Standing under the shower I let the cool, clear water wash the caked dust from my body, the chaotic scenes of the procession from my mind. Suddenly I am paralyzed by fear. This is the last time I will embrace my children, or laugh with my brother. The last time I will enjoy the privacy of my bathroom.

A servant is knocking at the bathroom door. "The barber has arrived. Your father is calling for you."

I abandon all hope of retreat. The ceremonies of renunciation have progressed too far. I wrap a towel around my waist and come out to join the barber. Seven monks are sitting cross-legged in a row outside the room.

I place my head before the barber and he starts cutting my thick hair. As the wet locks fall on the floor around me, the monks recite the afflictions I will endure when I become a member of their brotherhood.

"You will be a social outcast.

"You will be insulted.

"You will be hounded."

My father is weeping and I can hear my brother coughing, trying to restrain his emotion as the barber shaves my scalp.

"You will depend on strangers for your most basic needs.

"They will despise your weakness that imposes on their charity.

"You will be heartsick."

The barber finishes shaving my head, and I put my hand up to make sure he has left the five hairs intact that I will require at the diksha ceremony.

"You will experience cold.

"Hunger.

"Heat.

"Thirst.

"Sickness."

The bare skin of my scalp feels strange under my hand. I can feel it prickling in fear as the monks recite their litany of afflictions, preparing me for the future. I look at my father but he averts his eyes. Neither he nor I can any longer avoid the reality of my renunciation, and I cannot tell him now that I should have heeded his warnings.

"You will suffer pain from constant walking.

"You will suffer loneliness.

"You will grieve for your children.

"You will be deprived of the ministrations of any woman lest she arouse your desire."

My father's personality seems to undergo a change as he listens to the chanting. After the excesses of the procession he is subdued, sitting with me all night but at a distance, as if already awed by my new role and the relentless reminders of the masked monks in the darkness outside my chambers.

He leaves me only when he has to return to the stadium to preside over the feast he has organized for the massive congregation.

Now the monks hand me a muslin mask to tie over my mouth. They give me the three pieces of cloth that will be my only garments from today, and I go into the bathroom to change. In the mirror I examine my reflection for the last time. Seeing the five hairs hanging from my shaved scalp, I know I do not have the strength to endure the deprivations of my new life. For a long time I stand there, my forehead pressed against the marble walls of the bathroom.

When I finally come out the old monk gives me a stick tied with woolen tufts to clear my path and a wooden begging bowl, and we climb into the cars waiting to take us to the stadium.

At the gate the monks leave me. Still chanting, they file toward the podium where only twenty-four hours ago I commenced my departure from my father's world.

My father comes to fetch me. Seeing me in the garments of a mendicant, he weeps again, but I can offer him no consolation. I touch his feet as a son for the last time and enter the stadium.

The crowds are silent, watching my approach. I cannot believe it is the same place or that these are the same people from yesterday. There is an atmosphere of tense expectation as I walk around the stadium. It takes me a long time, and I can hear the sound of my bare feet on the baked mud of the field as the crowds fold their hands to me in hushed respect.

At last I climb the podium steps to join the chanting monks. Suddenly the stadium explodes in applause. People are on their feet, clapping and shouting encouragement. For half an hour I stand before them their cheers pounding in my ears. Once more I descend to circle the field, seeking again the blessings of these thousands of spectators to my act of renunciation.

They are still cheering when I return to the podium. Now the monks take my staff and begging bowl. I raise my hands to my shaved head. A silence descends on the stadium as I prepare to imitate Mahavira's last gesture against vanity.

One by one I pull out the long hairs left by the barber, gritting my teeth against the pain. I can feel the blood trickling down my scalp. Each time I wrench my hand away from my scalp, the crowd screams as if sharing my agony.

The monks enclose me in a circle until the crowd no longer knows which of us has renounced the world today. In that closed circle I can hear the monks chanting:

"You will be free from doubt.

"You will be free from delusion.

"You will be free from extremes.

"You will promote stability.

"You will protect life."

My father is looking for me but he will not find me. I have become a stranger, my features hidden behind a muslin mask.

And now, my friend, my brother monks are waiting for me in Mahadeo.

No, I cannot stay longer. You must find someone else to answer your questions.

If I am late, they will leave and I shall have to join a new sect of mendicants.

Don't ask me to do this, my friend.

I am too poor to renounce the world twice.

CHAPTER THREE

For some time the memory of the monk disturbs me. When I sit on the terrace before sunrise with my face turned toward the source of the river, I find I cannot concentrate, seeing the monk's intense eyes above the white mask covering his mouth as clearly as if a photographic image is being projected onto the darkness.

In the silence I can hear waves lapping at the riverbanks and I think of the ascetics meditating by the holy pool at Amarkantak, seeking through their meditations to liberate themselves from the cycle of rebirth and death.

At this hour I have sometimes seen the dull glow of something being swept downstream and known it was the corpse of an ascetic thrown into the river with a live coal burning in its mouth. I cannot stop myself from wondering if some day while I am sitting here in the dark I will see the monk's body floating beneath the terrace.

On entering the jungle for my morning walk, I loiter under the trees until it is time to visit Tariq Mia, anxious to avoid the caves for fear of finding myself in conversation with another stranger. To dispel my morbid thoughts I admire the red blossoms shaken from the flame trees by clambering monkeys. Or I pause between the branches rooted in the soil around an immense banyan tree like pillars in an ancient temple to watch birds guarding their nests from the squirrels streaking through the flat leaves.

By the time I climb the summit of the hill, my preoccupation with the monk begins to evaporate like the dew receding all around me in the sunlight. On the far bank of the river the morning sun is striking the canals that irrigate the fields, and I can see farmers moving behind their buffaloes through flourishing crops interlaced by silver ribbons of water.

Now I am full of anticipation at being with my friend. Although Tariq Mia often teases me, sometimes even suggesting I am pretentious, there is a lightness to my step as I descend into the valley that separates us.

A narrow bridge spans the stream that flows past Tariq Mia's mosque. Extending on one side of the mosque is a marble platform leading to the sixteenth-century tomb of the Sufi poet and saint Amir Rumi. Another platform leads to Tariq Mia's residence. Behind the mosque the whitewashed village houses form a pleasant jigsaw up the incline of the hill.

There is a placidness to the scene that suggests the calm of simple lives ordered only by the passing of the seasons and the call to prayer.

But once a year the calm is broken by Sufi singers from all over India who congregate at Amir Rumi's tomb to pay homage to their saint and poet on the anniversary of his death. For ten days and nights the marble platforms are covered with carpets, campfires flicker on the hillside, the hills echo to ecstatic singing. Then the singers are gone and Tariq Mia's mosque is enclosed once more in its habitual tranquility.

Today, by the time I reach Tariq Mia's house, the cane mats are already unrolled on his veranda, the bolster pillows propped against the pillars, and on a small wooden table the chess pieces have been readied for our game.

Tariq Mia stands on tiptoe to kiss my cheeks, his thin white beard brushing my chin. "What an unexpected pleasure! How surprised I was to see you on the bridge!"

A young divinity student with the scholar's black cap on his head enters the veranda with a tea tray. Tariq Mia is an acknowledged Islamic scholar, and there are always young clerics studying under him. I can see the student trying to hide his grin. I do the same. We both know Tariq Mia enjoys the solemn ritual of surprise although he watches for me every day.

"You should not have troubled to order tea. Your students will resent me for delaying their instruction."

"My students will thank Allah for their good fortune, knowing they must endure me the rest of the day. Come, little brother, bring your cup to the chess board."

Although I am past middle age, Tariq Mia is nearly eighty years old so I am not offended that he calls me "little brother," or that at the chess board he often conducts a gentle tutorial as if I, too, am his pupil.

The old mullah seems able to read my mind. If I am downcast he will suddenly banish my gloom by breaking into song. Too conscious of my own dignity, I never fail to be moved by the uninhibited delight in that quavering voice as he sings his Sufi songs of love to God.

"My heart is tangled in the locks of Your hair.
I swoon in the gaze of Your narcissus eyes.
My whole being circles You.
Can't You see my blood turning into henna
To decorate the soles of Your feet?"

Or he will tell me stories while he waits for me to move a knight. I concentrate so hard on evading capture, I do not grasp what he has told me until I am retracing my path to the bungalow.

In our early encounters I could not see the pattern in Tariq Mia's musings, attributing them to the changes of mood brought on by his age. Now, when he stares at the chessboard for too long I know those eyes, as alert as a panther's in that lined face, are about to fix on me, and I affectionately watch creases appearing on the high forehead above the hooked nose, already reconciled to my checkmate.

Today Tariq Mia is not pleased by my gloomy thoughts about dead ascetics.

"India's greatest poet also floated down this river," he remarks with some acerbity. "Kabir, the man whose poems made a bridge between your faith and mine. Meditate on Kabir's toothbrush. You will find it more useful than thinking about an ascetic's corpse."

Dismayed by Tariq Mia's disapproval, I confess that I have never heard of Kabir's toothbrush.

He shakes his head in irritation. "Don't you know the story? How Kabir was sailing down the Narmada, cleaning his teeth with a twig? He threw the twig onto a mud flat in the river. The twig put down roots and grew into a huge tree, the Kabirvad. Poets and singers and mystics have come from all over India to praise God by his many names under the shade of the Kabirvad, even in the worst times of religious slaughter."

Then Tariq Mia asks me why I am suddenly so concerned with ascetics. I tell him about my encounter. Tariq Mia is too wise to question my distraction over the Jain monk. He keeps his eyes firmly on the chessboard, allowing me to reveal the monk's story as I recollect it until I surprise myself by discovering the source of my confusion.

"The fault was mine, I suppose. I was so fascinated by his lavish renunciation ceremonies that I never asked him to explain his first words, 'I have loved only one thing in my life.' Now he has gone without telling me what it was."

At last Tariq Mia raises his eyes from the chessboard. "But of course he told you."

"What was it? The prayer of the Hindu ascetic who asks for eyes in the soles of his feet so he can keep his own eyes on the face of God?"

Tariq Mia puckers his lips in disappointment. "He followed in the footsteps of a man, not a god. What good would eyes in the soles of his feet be?"

I plead with Tariq Mia not to play with me and tell me what the Jain monk loved.

"The human heart, little brother. Its secrets."

"What secrets?"

"The human heart has only one secret. The capacity to love."

Seeing my perplexed expression, Tariq Mia sighs. "Oh, little brother, are you so unfortunate? Have you never been scalded by love?"

I consider the question. I know I was a dutiful son. As for my wife, she was a familiar presence in my house and in my bed, but I had no recollection of burning desire.

"Children! Come here, children!"

Tariq Mia's call brings two young scholars running into the veranda, their loose white pajamas flapping at their ankles.

"Fetch the gramophone. You will find it on top of the green almirah. There is a record in a brown folder on top of the gramophone. Don't drop it. The gramophone needles are in a box in my desk."

Tariq Mia lays a thin hand over mine. The skin is so transparent I can see the pulsing veins beneath as we wait for the students to return with the gramophone.

A scholar hands Tariq Mia an old brown folder, and he releases my hand to slide the record from its cover. He gently polishes the vinyl disc with his sleeve while the students crank the gramophone and fix a new steel needle into the ancient arm.

The turntable revolves, then a high voice pierces the morning silence.

"I prostrate my head to Your drawn sword.
    O, the wonder of Your kindness.
    O, the wonder of my submission

"In the very spasm of death I see Your face.
    O, the wonder of Your protection.
    O, the wonder of my submission."

The clarity of the voice, even through the hissing of the old record, is so extraordinary, each note hanging in the stillness like a drop of water, that it is some time before I decipher the savagery of the lyrics.

"Do not reveal the Truth in a world where
    blasphemy prevails.
      O wondrous Source of Mystery.
      O, Knower of Secrets.

"I bare my neck to Your naked blade.
O, the wonder of Your guidance.
O, the wonder of my submission."

Seeing my reaction to the song, Tariq Mia laughs and removes the arm from the record. "Drink some tea, little brother. How can you say you have given up the world when you know so little of it?"

He places a fresh cup of tea by my side. For a moment he stands at the edge of the veranda watching the water flowing under the bridge. Then he turns back to me. "Let me tell you another story, little brother. Perhaps it will help you understand the ways of the human heart."

He walks back to the chess table and slowly lowers himself onto his cushion. "This tale begins two years ago during the festival that celebrates the anniversary of Amir Rumi's death. I am an old man and can no longer keep vigil with the ecstasies of our Quawwali singers. You know how they can continue all night—nine, ten singers at a time. When one tires the other takes the song, inebriating them all with his devotion until they become drunk with singing and no longer remember fatigue in their praise of God."

I nod in understanding. Tariq Mia often speaks to me about the ecstatic songs of the Sufis, which can even move their listeners to dance with religious rapture.

"But, as I say, I am an old man and too close to meeting God myself to exhaust what little energy remains to me in singing to him all night, so I was fast asleep in my bed, my dreams filled with the richness of the music, too tired to hear the knocking at my window. Also, it was not a loud banging, just an insistent tapping on the glass that must have been going on for some time before it finally woke me.

"I opened my eyes and saw a face peering at me through the glass. I reluctantly got out of my bed to open the window. A man was standing outside, dressed in a close-collared jacket and a white dhoti. His thin gray hair was receding from his forehead and heavy-rimmed spectacles magnified the frightened expression in his brown eyes as he apologized again and again for disturbing my rest.

"It was some time before I was able to convince him to come inside. When at last he entered my room, I lit the lantern and poured him a glass of water, unable to understand why he was here. From his dress I could see he was not from this part of the country. Also, grief seemed to seep through his clothing although he was not weeping. I urged him to tell me what was troubling him.

" 'The boy!' he whispered.

" 'Your son? Have you lost your son in these hills?'

"He handed me a record, saying 'The boy always wanted to sing at the tomb of Amir Rumi.'

" 'How can I help you unless you tell me what has happened?'

" 'No one can help me. I am a murderer. But I must give the boy's music to Amir Rumi. Can you do this for me?'

"I took the record, assuring him I would see it was treasured as a valued offering to the saint's memory.

"He looked relieved and I could see the gentleness in his eyes. Thinking to ease the man's mind a little, I encouraged him to tell me about the crime of which he accused himself.

"Perhaps it was the lateness of the hour, or the ecstasy of the singers pouring through the open window, which gave him the strength to speak. But once he began it was as if he could not halt himself."

CHAPTER FOUR

THE TEACHER'S STORY

Master Mohan was not a bitter man. Although he led an unhappy life, his gentle nature disposed him to small acts of kindness—helping a stranger to dismount from a rickshaw, reaching into his pockets to find a boiled sweet for a child—and when he walked down the narrow streets leading to the avenue where he boarded the tram that took him to his music students, he was greeted warmly by the neighbors sitting on their tiny verandas to catch the breeze.

"Good evening, Master Mohan."

"A late class tonight?"

"Walk under the streetlights coming home, Master Mohan. These days one must be careful."

Near the tram stop, the paanwallah smearing

lime paste onto his paan leaves always shouted from inside his wooden stall, "Master! Master! Let me give you a paan. A little betel leaf will help you through the pain of hearing your students sing."

Even though it meant losing his place on the queue, Master Mohan stopped to talk to the paan-wallah and listen to his gossip of the comings and goings in the quarter. And so he was the first to learn the great Quawwali singers from Nizamud-din were coming to Calcutta.

"You should ask Mohammed-sahib to go with you. You are a teacher of music, he is a lover of poetry. And they are singing so close, in that mosque on the other side of the bazaar."

"But my wife will not go even that far to hear—"

"Wives! Don't talk to me of wives. I never take mine anywhere. Nothing destroys a man's pleasure like a wife."

Master Mohan knew the paanwallah was being kind. His wife's contempt for him was no secret on their street. The small houses were built on top of each other, and his wife never bothered to lower her voice. Everyone knew she had come from a wealthier family than his and could barely survive on the money he brought back from his music lessons.

"What sins did I commit in my last life that I

should be yoked to this apology for a man? See how you are still called Master Mohan as if you were only ten years old. Gupta-sahib you should be called. But who respects you enough to make even that small effort!"

Her taunts reopened a wound that might have healed if only Master Mohan's wife had left him alone. The music teacher had acquired the name as a child singer when he had filled concert halls with admirers applauding the purity of his voice. His father, himself a music teacher, had saved every paisa from his earnings to spend on Master Mohan's training, praying his son's future would be secured with a recording contract.

But it takes a very long time for a poor music teacher to cultivate connections with the owners of recording studios. For four years Master Mohan's father had pleaded for assistance from the wealthy families at whose houses his son sang on the occasion of a wedding or a birthday. For four years he had stood outside recording studios, muffling his coughs as tuberculosis ate away at his lungs, willing himself to stay alive until his son's talent was recognized, urging the boy to practice for that first record which would surely astonish the world.

When the recording contract was finally offered, only weeks before the record was to be made, Master Mohan's voice had broken.

Every day his wife reminded him how his voice had not mellowed in the years that followed. "Your family has the evil eye. Whatever you touch is cursed, whatever you are given you lose."

Sometimes Master Mohan tried to escape his wife's taunts by reminding himself of those four years of happiness that had preceded the moment when the golden bowl of his voice had shattered and with it his life. As her shrill insults went on and on, drilling into his brain, he found himself only able to remember his father's anguish that his son would have to abandon a great career as a singer, becoming just another music teacher like himself.

Master Mohan's father had made one last effort to help his son by engaging him in marriage to the daughter of a rich village landowner who loved music. He had lived long enough to see the marriage performed but not long enough to celebrate the birth of his two grandchildren, or to witness the avarice of his daughter-in-law when her own father died and her brothers took the family wealth, leaving her dependent on Master Mohan's earnings.

Prevented by pride from criticizing her family, Master Mohan's wife had held her husband responsible for the treachery of her brothers, raising their children to believe it was only Master

Mohan's weakness and stupidity that had robbed them of the servants, the cars, the fancy clothes from foreign countries that should have been their right.

"How can I ever forgive myself for burdening you with this sorry creature for a father? Come, Babloo, come, Dolly. Have some fruit. Let him make his own tea."

With such exactitude had she perfected her cruelty that Master Mohan's children despised their father's music as they despised him, allying themselves with their mother's neglect.

After giving music lessons all day Master Mohan was left to cook a meager meal for himself, which he took up to the small roof terrace of the house to escape his household's contempt. But he could not escape the blaring film music from the radio, or the loud noise of the gramophone echoing up the narrow stone stairwell leading to the terrace. It set him coughing, sometimes so loudly that his wife, or his daughter and son, would run up the stairs yelling at him to be quiet. Though he tried Master Mohan could not stop coughing. It was a nervous reaction to his family's ability to silence the music he heard in his own head.

So when the paanwallah told him about the Quawwali singers, Master Mohan found himself daydreaming on the tram. He had never heard the singers from Nizamuddin where Quawwali music had been born seven hundred years ago. But he knew Nizamuddin had been the fountain from which the poems and songs of the great Sufi mystics had flowed throughout India, and that even today its teachers still trained the finest Quawwali musicians in the country. He could not believe his good fortune—seven nights spent away from his wife and children listening to their music. And what is more, the music could be heard free.

On his way home that evening he stopped outside Mohammed-sahib's house. Finding him on his veranda, Master Mohan asked shyly if he would be listening to the Quawwali singers.

"Only if you accompany me. I am a poor fool who never knows what he is hearing unless it is explained to him."

So it was settled, and the next week Master Mohan hardly heard his wife and children shouting at him as he cooked himself a simple meal, relishing the taste of it while they listened to their noisy film music.

"Make sure you do not wake up the whole house when you return!" his wife shouted behind him as he slipped into the street.

By the time Master Mohan and Mohammed-sahib reached the tent tethered to one side of the mosque, the singing had begun and curious bazaar children crowded at the entrances.

Mohammed-sahib peered over their heads in disappointment. "We are too late. There is nowhere for us to sit."

Master Mohan refused to give up so easily. He squeezed past the children to look for a vacant place in the tent filled with people listening in rapt attention to the passionate devotional music breaking in waves over their heads.

He felt a familiar excitement as he led his friend to a small gap between the rows of people crushed against each other on the floor. The fluorescent lights winking from the struts supporting the tent, the musty odor of the cotton carpets covering the ground brought back the concerts of his childhood, and a constriction inside himself began to loosen.

On the podium nine performers sat cross-legged in a semicircle around a harmonium and a pair of tablas. An old sheikh from Nizamuddin sat to one side, his white beard disappearing into the loose robes flowing around him. Every now and then a spectator, moved by the music, handed the sheikh money, which he received as an offering to God before placing it near the tabla drums sending their throbbing beat into the night.

The more the singers were carried away by their music, the more Master Mohan felt the weight that burdened him lighten, as if the ecstasy of the song being relayed from one throat to another was lifting him into a long-forgotten ecstasy himself.

Twice Mohammed-sahib got up to place money at the sheikh's feet. Master Mohan watched him stepping over crossed legs as he made his way to stage, ashamed his own poverty prevented him from expressing gratitude to the singers for reviving emotions that he had thought dead.

After two hours Mohammed-sahib's funds and patience were exhausted, and he went home. Gradually the tent began to empty until only a few beggar children remained, asleep on the cotton carpets. Master Mohan looked at his watch. It was three o'clock in the morning.

In front of Master Mohan a young woman holding the hand of a child suddenly approached the podium to whisper to the sheikh. The sheikh leaned across to the singers wiping perspiration from their foreheads.

The lead singer nodded wearily and the young woman pulled the child behind her up the stairs. The boy stumbled twice, struggling to recover his balance. Then he was on the podium, both hands stretched in front of him. Master Mohan realized the boy was blind as the woman pushed him down next to the singers.

The lead singer sang a verse. The other singers took up the chorus. The lead singer sang another verse, his arm extended to the boy who could not see him. The singers prodded him and the startled child entered the song two octaves above the others.

"I prostrate my head to the blade of Your sword.
   O, the wonder of my submission.
   O, the wonder of Your protection."

It was a sound Master Mohan had only heard in his dreams.

"In the very spasm of death I see Your face.
   O, the wonder of Your protection.
   O, the wonder of my submission."

Until this moment he had believed such purity of tone was something that could only be imagined but never realized by the human voice.

He crept forward until he was sitting by the young woman.

"Who is that child?" he asked.

The young woman turned a pleasant face

pinched by worry to him. "My brother, Imrat. This is the first song my father taught Imrat—the song of the children of the Nizamuddin Quaw-wali."

Tears glistened in the large eyes. Under the fluorescent lights Master Mohan thought they magnified her eyes into immense pearls. "Last year I brought Imrat with me to Calcutta to sell my embroidery. While we were here, terrible floods swept our village away. Our father, my husband, everybody was killed."

Master Mohan glanced at the stage. The singers were already intoxicated by the power of their combined voices, unable to distinguish the singular voice of the child from all the other voices praising God.

"Do not reveal the Truth in a world where
blasphemy prevails.
O wondrous Source of Mystery.
O Knower of Secrets."

The woman covered her face with her hands. "I have been promised a job as a maidservant with a family who are leaving for the north of India, but I cannot take my brother because he is blind. I hope the sheikh will take Imrat to Nizamuddin until I can earn enough to send for him."

Master Mohan felt tears welling in his own eyes as he heard the high voice sing,

"I prostrate my head to the blade of Your
    sword.
        O, the wonder of Your guidance.
        O, the wonder of my submission."

The next evening Mohammed-sahib confessed, "I am not as musical as you, Master. God will forgive me for not accompanying you tonight."

So Master Mohan went alone to hear the Quawwali singers. The young woman and the blind child were sitting under the podium, still there when the other spectators had gone.

He waited all evening, hoping to hear the child's pure voice again, but that night the boy did not join the singers on the stage. The following night and the next, Master Mohan was disappointed to see the young woman and her brother were not present at the Quawwali.

On the fourth night Master Mohan found himself the last listener to leave the tent. As he hurried through the deserted alleys of the dark bazaar, he heard someone calling behind him, "Sahib, wait. For the love of Allah, listen to us."

He turned under the solitary street lamp at the end of the bazaar. The woman was pulling the child past the shuttered shops toward him.

"Please, sahib. The Quawwali singers are traveling around India. They cannot take my brother with them, and in two days I must start work or lose my job. You have a kind face, sahib. Can you keep Imrat? He is a willing worker. He will do the sweeping or chop your vegetables. Just feed him and give him a place to sleep until I can send for him."

A drunk stumbled toward the street lamp. "What's the woman's price, pimp? Offer me a bargain. She won't find another customer tonight."

The woman shrank into the darkness clutching the child in her arms. "For the love of Allah, sahib. Help us. We have nowhere to turn."

To his astonishment Master Mohan heard himself saying "I am a music teacher. I will take your brother as my pupil. Now you must return to the safety of the mosque."

The woman turned obediently into the dark alley. Master Mohan was grateful she could not see the expression on his face, or she must surely have recognized his fear at the offer he had made.

At the entrance to the tent he said, "I will come tomorrow evening to fetch the child."

The woman turned her face away to hide her

gratitude, whispering "Please, sahib, I have a last request. See my brother follows the practices of Islam."

The next morning Master Mohan went to the corner of the avenue to consult the paanwallah.

"You did what, Master? Do you know what your wife and children will do to that poor boy?"

"They would not harm a defenseless child!"

"Your wife will never permit you to keep the boy. Make some excuse to the sister. Get out of it somehow."

As they argued Mohammed-sahib joined them.

"I couldn't help myself," Master Mohan pleaded. "The girl was crying. If she loses her job, how will she feed herself and a blind brother? This is no city for a young woman alone."

Mohammed-sahib pulled at his mustache. "You have done a very fine thing, my friend. Prohibit your wife from interfering in your affairs. It is you who feed and clothe your family and put a roof over their heads. Your decision as to who shall share that roof is final and irreversible." He slapped Master Mohan on the back and turned toward the tram stop.

The paanwallah shook his head. "That fellow is as puffed up as a peacock. It is easy for him to give advice when it costs him nothing. Don't go back for the child, Master."

But Master Mohan could not betray the young woman's trust, even when he returned to the tent that night and saw the sobbing boy clinging to his sister's legs. Master Mohan lifted the weeping child in his arms as the sister consoled her brother. "I'll write often. Study hard with your kind teacher until I send for you. You'll hardly notice the time until we are together again."

The child was asleep by the time Master Mohan reached his silent household. He crept up the stone stairs to the terrace and laid Imrat on the cloth mattress, pleased when the child rolled over onto his torn shawl and continued sleeping.

Well, you can imagine how his wife shrieked the next morning when she discovered what Master Mohan had done. As the days passed her rage did not diminish. In fact, it got worse. Each day Master Mohan returned from giving his music lessons in the city to find his wife waiting for him on the doorstep with fresh accusations about the blind boy's insolence, his clumsiness, his greed. She carried her attack into the kitchen when Master Mohan was trying to cook food for himself and Imrat, chasing behind him up the narrow stairwell so that everyone could hear her abuse raging over the rooftops.

When Master Mohan continued to refuse her demand that Imrat be thrown out into the street,

Dolly and Babloo triumphantly joined in their mother's battle, complaining they no longer got enough to eat with another mouth sharing their food. In the evenings they placed their gramophone on the very top step of the stone staircase just outside the terrace, so the child could not hear the fragile drone of Master Mohan's tanpura strings giving the key for Imrat's music lesson. They teased Imrat by withholding his sister's letters, sometimes even tearing them up before Master Mohan had returned to the house and was able to read them to the waiting child.

Somehow Master Mohan discovered a strength in himself equal to his family's cruelty to Imrat. He arranged for the child's letters to be left with the paanwallah, and on the rare occasions when he entered the house and found his family gone to visit friends, he gently encouraged Imrat to stop cowering against the walls and become a child again. He would cook some special dish, letting the boy join in the preparations, encouraging him to eat his fill. Then he would take the child onto the roof terrace. After allowing his fingers to play over the strings of his tanpura until he found the note best suited to the boy's range, Master Mohan would ask Imrat to sing.

Hearing the clear notes pierce the night, Master Mohan knew he had been made guardian of something rare, as if his own life until now had only been a purification to ready him for the task of tending this voice for the world.

Then one day the music teacher returned late from giving a music lesson and found his daughter holding Imrat down while his son tried to force pork into the child's mouth. The child's sightless eyes were wide open, tears streaming down his cheeks. For the first time in his life Master Mohan struck his children. "He's only nine years old. How can you torture a child so much younger than yourselves! Get out of this house until you learn civilized behavior!"

With those words war was declared in Master Mohan's household. His wife accused Master Mohan of striking his own children out of preference for a blind beggar, unleashing such furious threats at the child that Master Mohan was worried Imrat would run away.

Mohammed-sahib would not agree to let Imrat live in his house, despite the music teacher's eloquent pleading. As he listened to Mohammed-sahib's elaborate excuses, Master Mohan realized his friend wished to avoid the unpleasantness of dealing with his wife.

"I warned you, Master," the paanwallah said with satisfaction when he heard of Mohammed-sahib's response. "That man is just good for free advice. Now there is only one thing to do. Go to the park in the early mornings. Only goats and shepherds will disturb you there. Don't give up, Master. After all, there is a whole world in which to practice, away from the distractions of your house."

So the music teacher woke his young charge before dawn and they boarded the first tram of the morning to reach the great park that is the center of Calcutta city.

When they arrived at the park, Master Mohan led Imrat by the hand between the homeless men and women wrapped in tattered cloths asleep under the great English oaks turning red each time the neon signs flashed, past the goatherds gossiping by their aluminum canisters until it was time to milk the goats grazing on the grass, toward the white balustrades that enclosed the marble mausoleum of the Victoria Memorial.

The music teacher lowered his cane mat and his tanpura over the side of the balustrade before gently lifting Imrat onto the wall. After climbing over himself, he lifted the child down, both so silent in the dark the guard asleep in his sentry box was left undisturbed.

With a swishing sound Master Mohan unrolled

his cane mat, still smelling of green fields, and seated Imrat next to him.

Then he played the first notes of the morning raga on his tanpura. To his delight, Imrat repeated the scale faultlessly.

Master Mohan explained the significance of the raga, initiating Imrat into the mystery of the world's rebirth, when light disperses darkness and Vishnu rises from his slumbers to redream the universe.

Again Imrat sang the scale, but there was a new resonance in his voice. He could not see the faint blur of the picket fences ringing the race course in the distance, or the summit of Ochterlony's Needle breaking through the smoke from the illegal fires built by the street hawkers around the base of the obelisk. He could not even see the guard looking through his sentry box, his hand half raised to expel them from the gardens, frozen in that gesture by the boy's voice. He only saw the power of the morning raga and, dreaming visions of light, he pushed his voice toward them, believing sight was only a half tone away.

Afraid the raga would strain the child's voice, Master Mohan asked Imrat to sing a devotional song. The boy obediently turned his head toward the warmth of the sun's first rays and sang,

"The heat of Your presence
    Blinds my eyes.
    Blisters my skin.
    Shrivels my flesh.

"Do not turn in loathing from me.
    O Beloved, can You not see
    Only Love disfigures me?"

Master Mohan patted Imrat's head. "That is a beautiful prayer. Where did you learn such a song?"

Tears clouded the clouded eyes. "It is a poem by Amir Rumi. My father said that one day he and I would sing it at Amir Rumi's tomb together."

The music teacher took the child in his arms. "You will still sing at Amir Rumi's tomb, I promise you. And your father will hear your voice from heaven. Come, sing it once more so I can listen properly."

The child blew his nose and again shocked the music teacher with power of his voice.

"Do not turn in loathing from me.
    O Beloved, can You not see
    Only Love disfigures me?"

At that moment a sudden belief took root in Master Mohan's mind. He was convinced God was giving him a second voice, greater than he had ever heard, greater than his own could ever have been. He was certain such a voice must only be used to praise God, lest fate exact a second revenge by robbing him of it.

Sure of his purpose as a teacher at last, Master Mohan asked the boy, "Did your father ever teach you the prayers of Kabir? Do you know this hymn?"

He played some notes on his tanpura and Imrat responded with excitement, opening his throat full to contain the mystic's joy.

"O servant, where do you seek Me?
You will not find Me in temple or mosque,
In Kaaba or in Kailash,
In yoga or renunciation.

"Sings Kabir, 'O seeker, find God
In the breath of all breathing.' "

And now a most extraordinary thing happened. Someone threw a coin over the wall, and it fell on the grass in front of Master Mohan. The music teacher stood up. On the other side of the balustrade, just visible in the first light of dawn, he saw a group of goatherds leaning on the wall.

By the next morning people were already waiting for them, and the guard waved Master Mohan and Imrat benevolently through the gate. Word had spread in the park that a blind boy with the voice of an angel was singing in the gardens of the Victoria Memorial. In the darkness goatherds, street hawkers, refugees with children huddled to their bodies, waited patiently for Imrat to practice the scales of the morning raga before Master Mohan permitted him to sing the devotional songs that would give them the endurance to confront the indignities of their lives for another day.

Morning after morning they listened to the music teacher instruct Imrat in the songs of Kabir and Mirabai, of Khusrau and Tulsidas, of Chisti and Chandidas, the wandering poets and mystics who had made India's soul visible to herself. Sometimes they even asked the boy to repeat a song, and Master Mohan could see them responding to the purity of the lyrics translated with such innocence by Imrat's voice.

To show their gratitude they began to leave small offerings on the wall above the balustrade: fruit, coins, a few crumpled rupees. And when the morning lesson ended, the street vendors crowded around Master Mohan and Imrat to offer a glass of steaming sweet tea or a hot samosa straight off a scalding iron pan.

Within a week Imrat's audience had expanded. Wealthy people on their morning walks stopped at the balustrade, drawn by the beauty of Imrat singing,

> "*Some seek God in Mecca,*
> *Some seek God in Benares.*
>> *Each finds his own path and the focus of*
> > *his worship.*

> "*Some worship Him in Mecca.*
> *Some in Benares.*
> > *But I center my worship on the eyebrow*
> > *of my Beloved.*"

Over the weeks more and more people made the balustrade part of their morning routines, until Master Mohan was able to recognize many faces at the wall, and every day he smiled at a young woman who folded a ten-rupee note, placing it in a crevice in the parapet.

When they dismounted from the tram, the paanwallah shouted his congratulations to fortify them against the raging wife waiting at the music teacher's house.

"Well, little Master Imrat. Your fame is spreading throughout Calcutta. Soon you will be rich. How much money did you make today?"

"Thirteen rupees." Imrat pulled the music teacher toward the sound of the paanwallah's voice. "How much have we got now?"

"Still a long way to go, Master Imrat. But here is another letter from your sister."

The paanwallah kept Imrat's money so Master Mohan's wife would not take it. It was Imrat's dream to earn enough money by his singing to live with his sister again, and each time she wrote he sang with renewed force.

Perhaps it was the fervor in Imrat's voice the morning after he had received another letter from his sister that made the miracle happen.

As Imrat was ending his song a man in blazer shouted, "Come on, come on, my good fellow. I haven't got all morning. Do you read English?"

The music teacher put down his tanpura and walked to the balustrade. The man handed him a paper without even looking at him, turning to the woman at his side. "Does the boy have a name or not? Can't sign a recording contract without a name."

Master Mohan pulled himself to his full height in defense of the child's dignity although the man in the blazer had his back to him. "He is blind and cannot read or write. But I am his guardian. I can sign for him."

"Jolly good. Turn up at the studio this afternoon so the engineers can do a preliminary test. That's what you want isn't it, Neena?"

His companion lifted her face and Master Mohan saw she was the woman who left ten rupees on the wall every day.

She smiled at Master Mohan's recognition. "Is this gifted child your son?"

Master Mohan shyly told her the story of Imrat, suppressing anything that might reflect well on himself, only praising the boy's talent. He could see the interest in her eyes, but the man was pulling at her elbow. "Fascinating, fascinating. Well, be sure to be at the studio at four o'clock. The address is on the contract."

Master Mohan studied the paper. "It says nothing here about payment."

"Payment?" For the first time the man in the blazer looked at him. "Singing for coppers in the park and you dare ask for payment?"

"We are not beggars." Master Mohan could not believe his own temerity. "I am a music teacher. I give the boy his lessons here so as not to disturb our household."

The woman laid her hand on the man's arm.

"Don't be such a bully, Ranjit. Offer him a thousand rupees. You'll see it is a good investment."

The man laughed indulgently. "You are the most demanding sister a man ever had. Here, give me that paper." He pulled a pen from his blazer and scribbled down the sum, signing his name after it.

Master Mohan folded the paper and put it carefully in his pocket. When he looked up he saw two men watching him from the other side of the wall. Their oiled hair and stained teeth frightened him, bringing back memories of the musicians who had waited outside the great houses where he had sung as a child, until the menfolk sent for the dancing girls who often did not even dance before musicians such as these led them to the bedrooms.

On their way home Imrat lifted his blind eyes to his teacher and whispered, "But how much money is a thousand rupees? Enough to find somewhere to live with you and my sister?"

The music teacher hugged the child. "If the record is a success you can be together with your sister. Now try and rest. This afternoon you must not be tired."

As they dismounted from the tram the paanwallah shouted, "Last night two musicians were asking about about you, Master. Did they come to hear Imrat today?"

Imrat interrupted the paanwallah. "We are going to make a record and get lots of money."

"A record, Master Imrat! Be sure you sing well. Then I will buy a gramophone to listen to you."

It was no surprise to Master Mohan that Imrat sang as he did that afternoon. The child could not see the microphone dangling from the wire covered with flies or the bored faces watching him behind the glass panel. He only saw himself in his sister's embrace, and when the recording engineer ordered him to sing the studio reverberated with his joy.

"The boy has recording genius," an engineer admitted reluctantly as Imrat ended his song. "His timing is so exact we can print these as they are."

His colleague switched off the microphone. "Ranjit-sahib will be very pleased. I'll call him."

A few minutes later the man in the blazer strode into the office followed by his engineers. "Well done, young man. Now my sister will give me some peace at last. She has done nothing but talk about you since she first heard you sing."

He patted Imrat's head. "Come back in ten days. If the engineers are right and we do not have to make another recording, I will give you a thousand rupees. What will a little chap like you do with so much money?"

But he was gone before Imrat could reply.

Master Mohan dared not hope for anything until the record was made. To prevent the child from believing too fervently that he would soon be reunited with his sister, the music teacher continued Imrat's lessons in the park, trying not to feel alarm when he saw the same two men always at the balustrade, smiling at him, nodding their heads in appreciation of Imrat's phrasing.

One day the men followed Master Mohan and Imrat to the tram, waiting until they were alone before approaching the music teacher with their offer.

"A great sahib wants to hear the boy sing."

"No, no. We are too busy." Master Mohan pushed Imrat before him. "The boy is making his first record. He must practice."

"Don't be a fool, brother. The sahib will pay handsomely to listen to his voice."

"Five thousand rupees, brother. Think of it."

"But your sahib can hear the child free every morning in the park."

They laughed and Master Mohan felt the old fear when he saw their betel-stained teeth. "Great men do not stand in a crowd, snatching their pleasure from the breeze, brother. They indulge their pleasures in the privacy of palaces."

"He must finish his recording first."

"Naturally. But after that . . ."

"We will be here every morning, Master."

"You will not escape us."

To Master Mohan's dismay the men waited each day at the park, leaning against the parapet until Imrat's small crowd of admirers had dispersed before edging up to the blind boy.

"Please, little Master Imrat, take pity on a man who worships music."

"The sahib's responsibilities prevented him from following his own calling as a singer."

"He could have been a great singer like you, Master Imrat, if he had not been forced to take care of his family business."

Master Mohan could see the smirking expressions on the faces of the two men as they tried to ingratiate themselves with Imrat.

"To hear you sing will relieve the pain of his own heart, denied what he has most loved in this life."

"If you sing well he will give you leaves from Tansen's tamarind tree to make your voice as immortal as Tansen's."

Master Mohan knew these men had once learned music as Imrat was doing now, until poverty had reduced them to pandering to the vices and whims of wealthy men. Even as he despised them he was relieved that Imrat's record would save him from such a life.

Now they turned their attention on Master Mohan.

"We have told the great sahib this boy has a voice that is heard only once in five hundred years."

"The sahib is a man of influence, brother. Perhaps he can arrange to have the boy invited to the Calcutta Music Festival."

The music teacher felt dizzy even imagining that his blind charge, who had been no better than a beggar only eight months ago, might be invited to sing in the company of India's maestros. The great singing teachers always attended the festival. One might even offer to train Imrat's pure voice, taking it to a perfection that had not been heard since Tansen himself sang before the Great Moghul. He nearly agreed but controlled himself enough to say again "You must wait until the boy completes his recording."

Fortunately he did not have to think long about the temptation offered by the two men.

On the day he took Imrat back to the recording studio, the young woman was also present in the office, seated on an armchair opposite her brother's desk.

"I played this record for the director of the radio station. He thinks Master Imrat has great promise, and must be taught by the best teachers available. A talent like his should not be exposed to the dust and germs in the park. There are empty rooms above one of our garages. He must live there."

The woman put her arm around boy. "Wouldn't you like to stay with me? Your sister could work in my house and your teacher would come to see you every day."

The boy nodded happily, and she handed two copies of the record and an envelope of money to Master Mohan. "So it is settled. As soon as his sister reaches Calcutta they will both move into my house."

Master Mohan took the records but left the envelope of money in the woman's hand for Imrat's sister.

"Are we to be given nothing for feeding and clothing this changeling you brought into our home?" Master Mohan's wife screamed when she learned her husband had left the boy's money with the studio owner. "What about the whole year we have kept him, restricting our own lives so he could become rich? Are your own children to receive nothing out of this, only blows and abuses?"

Her fury increased when Imrat's record was released and proved immediately popular.

In the weeks that followed, the record was played over and over again on the radio by enthusiastic programmers. While Imrat waited for his sister to send news of her arrival in Calcutta, Master Mohan was informed by the recording studio that Imrat's record was disappearing from the record shops as fast as new copies could be printed.

Now his wife's rage was inflamed by jealousy. She could hear Imrat's record being played everywhere in the bazaars. Even the paanwallah had brought a gramophone to his stall, storing it behind the piles of wet leaves at his side. Each time a customer bought a paan the paanwallah cranked the machine and placed the record on the turntable, boasting "I advised the music teacher to adopt the child. Even though he was only a blind beggar, I was able to recognize the purity of his voice immediately."

A week before Imrat's sister was due to arrive in Calcutta, the music teacher's wife learned from Mohammed-sahib that her husband had refused to let Imrat perform at the home of a great sahib.

"And he was offering the sum of five thousand rupees to listen to the blind boy," Mohammed-sahib said in awe.

"Five thousand rupees!" Master Mohan's wife

shrieked. "He turned down five thousand rupees when his own children do not have enough to eat and nothing to wear! Where can I find those men?"

That night the music teacher helped Imrat into the house. To his distress, he found his wife entertaining the two men who had come so often to the park.

She waved a sheaf of notes in Master Mohan's face. "I have agreed the brat will sing before the sahib tonight. See, they have already paid me. Five thousand rupees will cover a little of what I have spent on this blind beggar over the last year."

The music teacher tried to object but Imrat intruded on his arguments. "I am not tired, Master-sahib."

"Waited on hand and foot by our entire household! Why should you be tired?" She grabbed the boy's arm. "I'm coming myself to make sure you sing properly to pay for all the meals you have eaten at our table."

The two men smiled victoriously at the music teacher. "Our rickshaws are waiting at the corner of the street."

As they rode to the great sahib's house, Master Mohan felt tears on his cheeks. In a week Imrat would be gone, leaving him imprisoned again in his hateful household. He hugged Imrat to his chest, his sighs lost in the rasping breathing of the man straining between the wooden shafts of the rickshaw.

At the high iron gates of a mansion the rickshaws halted. A guard opened the gates and Master Mohan's wife seized Imrat's arm, pulling him roughly behind her as servants ushered them through a series of dimly lit chambers into a dark room empty of furniture.

Wooden shutters sealed the French doors on either side of the room, and large patches of paint peeled from the walls. The floor was covered by a Persian carpet that extended from the door to a raised platform. Above the platform two unused chandeliers hung from the ceiling, shrouded in muslin like corpses.

A man sat on the platform, his size exaggerated by the candles burning on either side of him. The musicians bowed to him obsequiously. The sahib ignored them. Still smiling, the musicians climbed onto the platform where a harmonium and drums were placed in readiness for the concert.

"Come here, little master," the great sahib said. "I am told you have a voice such as India has not heard for hundreds of years."

Master Mohan's wife released her hold on the boy, and the music teacher led him to the platform, grateful that Imrat could not see this empty room with its sealed wooden shutters and the shadows flickering on the peeling walls.

As he helped him up the stairs, the music teacher whispered in Imrat's ear, "Only sing the two songs from your record. Then we can go home."

"Soon I will be with my sister again," Imrat answered in a whisper as Master Mohan gently pushed him down in front of the two musicians. "Tonight I must thank Allah for his kindness."

For a few minutes only the music of the harmonium echoed through the heavy shadows of the room, and Master Mohan could feel his wife shifting restlessly from foot to foot at his side. Then Imrat's clear voice pierced the darkness.

"I prostrate my head to Your drawn sword.
        O, the wonder of Your kindness.
        O, the wonder of my submission.

"Do not reveal the Truth in a world where
        blasphemy prevails.
                O wondrous Source of Mystery.
                O Knower of Secrets."

The boy's sightless eyes seemed fixed on infinity, and it seemed to Master Mohan that the candles in the shrouded chandeliers were leaping into flame, ignited by Imrat's innocent devotion as he sang,

"In the very spasm of death I see Your face.
    O, the wonder of my submission.
    O, the wonder of Your protection."

Listening to the purity of each note, Master Mohan felt himself being lifted into another dimension, into the mystic raptures of the Sufis who were sometimes moved to dance by such music. For the first time he understood why the Sufis believed that once a man began to dance in the transport of his ecstasy, the singers must continue until the man stopped dancing lest the sudden breaking of the dancer's trance should kill him.

"The heat of Your presence
    Blinds my eyes.
    Blisters my skin.
    Shrivels my flesh."

The great sahib rose to his feet. Master Mohan wondered if the great sahib was about to dance as music poured out of that young throat which carried in it too great a knowledge of the world.

"The heat of Your presence
        Blinds my eyes.
        Blisters my skin.
        Shrivels my flesh

"Do not turn in loathing from me.
        O Beloved, can You not see
        Only Love disfigures me."

In the flickering light of the candles Master Mohan thought he saw something glint in the sahib's hand. The musicians were smiling ingratiatingly, waiting for the great sahib to circle the boy's head with money before flinging it to them. Now Master Mohan could not see Imrat, dwarfed by the shadow of the man standing in front of him as he sang again,

"I prostrate my head to Your drawn sword.
        O, the wonder of Your kindness.
        O, the wonder of my submission.

"Do not reveal the Truth in a world where
        blasphemy prevails.
        O wondrous Source of Mystery.
        O Knower of Secrets."

The great sahib turned around and Master Mohan thought he saw tears on his cheeks. "Such a voice is not human. What will happen to music if this is the standard by which God judges us?"

Imrat was not listening, intoxicated by the power issuing from his own throat.

"In the very spasm of death I see Your face.
  O, the wonder of my submission.
  O, the wonder of Your protection . . ."

Master Mohan could hear his wife cursing. He did not know his own screams echoed the blind boy's as he screamed and screamed and screamed.

CHAPTER FIVE

"What happened? Why was the music teacher screaming?"

"Wouldn't you scream if you saw a man slitting a boy's throat?"

"The great sahib killed the boy?" I asked in horror. "Why? Why would he do such a thing?"

"Why does a man steal an object of worship so no one but himself can enjoy it?"

"But did the police catch the great sahib?"

"Of course not. He was a rich man." Tariq Mia pushed the chess table aside and rose stiffly to his feet. "The two musicians were charged with the murder."

"What happened to Master Mohan?"

Tariq Mia bent over to remove the record from

the gramophone. "Oh, he lived here with me for several months. Eventually I convinced him he was not responsible for the boy's death. Then he left. Now, little brother, I must join my students."

I got up as Tariq Mia slid the record back into the old yellow folder. "Where did he go? Back to Calcutta? To his wife and children?"

Tariq Mia held the record out to me. "Would you like to take this home and listen to the boy's singing again?"

I was appalled by the suggestion. He laughed at my reaction. "You mustn't be so frightened of love, little brother."

Still chuckling at my distress, he took my arm and led me from the veranda, over the marble platform toward the bridge.

"What happened to the music teacher, Tariq Mia?" I persisted.

"He decided to return to his family. But he threw himself under the train before it reached Calcutta."

"Why?"

Tariq Mia stretched up to kiss my cheek, then gently pushed me onto the bridge. "Perhaps he could not exist without loving someone as he had loved the blind child. I don't know the answer, little brother. It is only a story about the human heart."

. . .

Crossing the bridge, I did not turn around to wave good-bye. I was upset by the old mullah's accusation that I did not understand the world. Especially, I told myself, when all Tariq Mia's knowledge of the world had not prevented the poor music teacher from taking his own life.

Loud laughter pierced the morning silence as I walked through the jungle back to the bungalow. The Vano village women were collecting fuel by the sides of the mud path.

Through the undergrowth I could see their slender brown arms reaching for the dry branches fallen on the mud. As I approached them I saw the saris sliding from their shoulders, baring their waists and the curve of their full breasts to my view as they stacked bundles of wood onto the small donkeys grazing under the trees.

The sturdy bodies of the village women, their catlike faces with the triangular tattoo marks high on each cheekbone, were such a relief after Tariq Mia's story that I returned their greetings with uncharacteristic warmth.

They nudged each other in surprise. "The sahib finds your face pretty today, Rano."

"It must be the season. Spring rouses even old tigers from their rest."

"It's true. Don't you see a prowl to the sahib's walk this morning?"

Their provocative laughter followed me down the gentle incline of the path. "Be careful not to walk alone, sisters. The mango trees are in bloom."

"Kama must be sharpening his arrows of blossoms and stringing his bow with bees, sisters. Take care the sahib does not lure us to a seduction."

I could not help smiling at the women's references to Kama, God of Love, with his sugarcane bow strung with honeybees and his five flowered arrows of desire. There was indeed a mood of longing in the jungle. Small flowers foamed over the leaves of the mango trees, the wind carried the scent of lemon blossoms and sandalwood to my nostrils.

The call of the koil bird, that strange imitation of a woman's cry at the moment of sexual fulfillment, hung suspended in the air, and I felt mythology might at any moment become reality. That Kama might suddenly draw his sugarcane bow, known as the Exciter of Madness, and unleash one of his five arrows on a hapless wanderer who would then crave some unsuspecting woman as an incarnation of Delight, the Goddess of Involuntary Allure. And to make sure of victory Kama might call on his friends—Spring with his ruthless hands and his beautiful body clothed only in lotus buds, or the Malayan Wind carrying the aromatic perfumes of the South, or most dangerous of all, Amorous Mood.

Grateful to the laughing women for lifting my gloom, I turned to wave at them but they had disappeared and only the green canopy of the jungle rustled over the hill.

Mr. Chagla leaned from the window of his office as I opened the small wooden gate at the back entrance to the bungalow. "Sir! Sir! One minute, sir."

He hurried into the garden, the slight roll to his gait emphasizing the endearing roundness of his whole appearance. Although Mr. Chagla bicycles a good two hours every day, from the town of Rudra to the bungalow and back again, his exertions seem to make little impression on his plump body or interfere with the genial innocence of his open nature, which finds delight in the smallest incident.

"The sugarcane men came while you were on your walk, sir."

"I'm sorry, Chagla. I was unavoidably detained at the mosque."

"Mention not, sir. I purchased three bundles. At this very time they are stacked against the kitchen wall. We will have lots of juice for the visitors."

He handed me a letter with the indulgence of a parent handing a child a toy and I felt his expectant gaze on my face as I read.

The letter was from an old colleague. "My nephew, Nitin Bose, will be coming to your bungalow for a few weeks' leave. He is interested in tribal customs. He is a very brilliant young man and has recently been made a director of a big tea company. Please keep an eye on him. I count on your understanding and discretion."

"Well, sir? Which suite shall I prepare?" Mr. Chagla's smile tightened the shining skin of his round face.

"The letter doesn't say when the visitor is arriving."

"We must prepare for all eventualities, sir. Shall I move in extra beds at least?"

"We are only expecting one young man. No mention is made of a wife or children." The brown eyes lost their bright anticipation and I added hurriedly, "But send me a glass of sugarcane juice while I read the post. If it is sweet enough, we'll buy some more to make cane sugar."

Cheered by an opportunity to give pleasure, Mr. Chagla moved toward the kitchen with his rolling walk.

My house had already been swept and dusted. The green-painted wooden shutters were open and the papers on my table rustled in the breeze. I sat down to work but found I could not concentrate on the list of accounts Mr. Chagla had prepared for my approval.

The teasing of the women had left me restless. Behind me I could hear the rushing of the waterfalls. I pushed the papers away and walked to the end of my small lawn to look down at the Narmada River.

At noon the sun is so strong its harsh light gives the river the appearance of beaten metal, but at this hour the morning light catches every nuance of the water's movement. Below me the wind was tossing the rippling waves up so that they sparkled in the light, before disappearing into the shadows below. I watched the water sparkling and disappearing, sparkling and disappearing, like the anklets encircling a woman's foot, and thought of the Ascetic watching the dancing woman formed by the rivulets from his own penance.

A flock of parakeets, messengers of Kama, God of Love, settled in a green cloud on the mango tree shading my head. I smiled, remembering how the

Ascetic had sneered at Kama's power, even though the gods had warned the Ascetic that he too must feel Desire for without Desire the play of the worlds would cease.

But still the Ascetic had sneered as he was pierced by the five flower-tipped arrows unleashed by Kama from his sugarcane bow—the Enchanter, the Inflamer, the Parcher, the Paroxysm of Desire, the Carrier of Death.

Then Maya, the Illusion of the Worlds, had appeared—the only woman capable of arousing the lust of the Destroyer of Worlds. Enraged at the destruction of his meditation, the Ascetic had opened his third eye, the Lotus of Command, and reduced Kama to ashes, even as he himself was being consumed by Desire.

Suddenly I was alarmed by the prospect of our new visitor. My colleague's letter had said his nephew was interested in tribal customs, but what did the young man really know about the beliefs of the tribals?

Did he know the goddess who had incinerated even the Great Ascetic in the fires of longing, the goddess whose power had been acknowledged by the ancient sages with such fearful names as the Terrible One, the Implacable Mother, the Dark Lady, the Destroyer of Time, the Everlasting Dream—did he know the goddess had been worshipped by the tribal inhabitants of these jungles for thousands of years?

Now the teasing of the Vano women seemed more threatening than Tariq Mia's tale of murder and suicide. Would a brilliant mind be enough to protect the young man from the dark forces of the jungles, from the tribal worship of that Desire which even their conquerors had acknowledged to be invincible, describing it as the firstborn seed of the mind?

"Sir, taste this." Mr. Chagla was standing at my side with a glass of sugarcane juice. "You will definitely find it up to the mark, sir."

His eager face smiled encouragingly at me, pulling me back into the day.

CHAPTER SIX

A full month passed before I heard from my colleague again. By then the clusters of mango blossoms had hardened into fruit and I had long forgotten my brief moment of anxiety.

Those varieties of mangoes not sweet enough to eat were already sliced and pickled, marinating in lemon juice in large glass jars on the ledge outside the pantry. Mr. Chagla had arranged for the delivery of bundles of sugarcane and I had myself stirred the boiling cane juice. Now there were enough hard rounds of brown cane sugar sitting in the dark, net-covered larder to last us through the monsoons.

Mr. Chagla laughed when I passed him the telegram from my old colleague, informing me that Nitin Bose was arriving by train the next day.

"We will have no juice for him, sahib. But don't worry. The cook will some way revive Mr. Bose from his dusty journey."

"Prepare the north suite, Chagla. Apparently our visitor is interested in the tribals. From his balcony he will be able to see Vano village. And when you return to Rudra make arrangements to meet the train."

The noise of a motorcycle roaring down the path behind the bungalow interrupted my instructions, and Mr. Chagla followed me across the garden.

"But this is Shashi, my school friend from so many years," Mr. Chagla announced in surprise as a constable from Rudra police station parked his motorcycle at the gate. "What can he want?"

"You will have to accompany me at once, sahib!" the constable shouted at me. "There has been some trouble with one of your visitors."

"But, Shashi, we have no visitors at all!" Mr. Chagla cried. "Who is creating such a mistake?"

"What can I do, Chagla? Your address was in his pocket. 'Care of the Narmada rest house.'"

"Shashi, you are not telling sense to my sahib. Who is this he? Where is this he?"

"In a cell at the police station in Rudra."

"A prisoner?" I asked.

"Well, that's the problem, sahib. We think he was trying to kill himself. We found him standing on the very edge of a cliff, staring down into the Narmada."

"Oof-oh. What a terrible thing!" Mr. Chagla shook his round head in dismay. "Was he going to jump in?"

"We are not sure of his real actual intentions. When we asked what he was doing there on the cliff he only said, 'Bring me my oil and my collyrium. Sister, bring the mirror and my vermilion.'"

Mr. Chagla stared at him dumbstruck. The constable looked away in embarrassment, and for a moment we all stood there in silence. Then Mr. Chagla recovered himself sufficiently to demand, "And his good name, Shashi. What is the poor fellow's good name?"

The constable turned to me, opening his hands in a gesture of helplessness. "That is another problem, sahib. He gives only a woman's name but he is most certainly a man."

I couldn't control my curiosity. "What name does he give?"

"Rima, sahib. We have confined him, but we have not charged him. How can we charge a man under the name of Miss Rima Bose?"

The telegram had informed us of the imminent

arrival of Nitin Bose. I remembered my old friend had ended his letter by saying he depended on my discretion. I wondered if the constable's prisoner was my colleague's nephew, and why my colleague hadn't warned me that his nephew was mad.

"Has your prisoner been seen by the doctor?"

The constable was affronted. "Of course, sahib. Very first thing. The doctor sent me to bring you. He says he can do nothing."

"But what is wrong with him?"

The constable lowered his voice and Mr. Chagla inclined his plump torso forward to listen more closely. "The prisoner told to the doctor that he is possessed."

Remounting his motorcycle, the constable waited for me to climb onto the pillion seat behind him. "Now, sahib, please hurry. My sergeant must be waiting so anxiously for your arrival."

Mr. Chagla unlocked the chain of his bicycle. "Don't be alarmed whatsoever, sir. Shashi is a capital driver, safe as anything. And I will be following close behind, to solve this mystery."

The wind whipped past my face, making my eyes water as we raced through the jungle toward Rudra. By the time the motorcycle bumped onto the tarmac road, my eyes were watering so badly the small painted houses were only a blur of lime-greens and blues connected by bougainvillea bushes and rows of black crows perched on electric wires.

The constable slowed down as we neared a square building with iron-barred windows. I recognized Dr. Mitra's spare frame leaning down to talk to a policeman at the entrance of the police station.

"My dear fellow, what a business." Dr. Mitra helped me off the motorcycle and led me up the concrete stairs. "I have just come back from the station with the poor chap's luggage. It was addressed to your bungalow. Were you expecting someone by the name of Nitin Bose?"

When he saw my expression he placed a lean arm around my shoulder. "Don't worry. It will soon be sorted out. In any case, the young man is not at all menacing. Come, see for yourself."

We passed the police desk and entered a corridor that led to a solitary cell at the back of the building. The police sergeant was sitting on an iron cot talking to a young man who was pacing silently up and down the cell.

The distinction of the young man surprised me. There was an air of authority to his carriage, and his well-cut cotton suit still flattered his body even though the cloth was creased. As he retraced his steps, through the stubble covering his dark skin I saw he had an aristocratic face with strong features.

The police sergeant got up wearily. "The prisoner won't talk to me, sahib. I can't even get him to admit his name is Nitin Bose."

Dr. Mitra gently pushed me into the cell. "You try talking to him. Perhaps you will have better luck than us. Say you were expecting him."

The sergeant followed Dr. Mitra down the corridor, leaving me alone with the young man.

"Your uncle and I were deputy secretaries at the same time," I began awkwardly. "In the Ministry of Agriculture. In fact, he sent me a telegram, saying I should expect you tomorrow. But you are already here."

I laughed nervously, unnerved by Nitin Bose's silence. "For two years our offices were adjacent. Right next to each other. Perhaps that is why he suggested you stay in our bungalow. . . ."

The young man suddenly gripped my shoulders. I was not frightened by the pressure of his fingers when I saw the fear deep in his eyes.

"You must help me," he whispered. "Read my diary. You will understand why I must find the shrine."

His voice broke and he sat down on the iron cot.

"What shrine?" I asked, moved by his desperation.

He struggled to control himself. When he was able to speak he answered, "They say there is a shrine to a goddess in these jungles. A tribal goddess, who cures the madness of those who are possessed. Can you help me find it?"

His request was so simple I almost started laughing again from sheer relief. The bitterness in his eyes stopped me and I said soberly, "Our bungalow guards worship at that shrine. They can take you there any time you wish."

"Then I must come with you."

I shook my head in alarm, unprepared to take responsibility for a man in his state. To my horror he knelt on the floor and seized my feet. "I will cause no trouble, I swear it. If I cannot visit the shrine I will have to kill myself. I can't go on like this."

I backed out of the cell. "Let me consult the doctor. We must abide by the doctor's advice."

A policeman came to lock the cell door as I hurried into the police sergeant's office, where Mr. Chagla was helping Dr. Mitra go through the young man's suitcase.

The police sergeant was describing each item to the constable, Shashi, who was carefully recording it in a lined ledger.

"Have you found a diary?" I asked. "He says it explains everything. And he wants to return to the rest house with me."

Mr. Chagla triumphantly handed me a leather-bound volume.

"Congratulations, my dear fellow." Dr. Mitra took my other hand between his bony fingers.

"For what?"

"You have brought the boy back to his senses. I knew it was a temporary aberration. He has probably been undergoing some severe emotional strain—overwork, an unhappy love affair, that sort of thing—and was suffering from momentary amnesia. I believe it happened to Agatha Christie once."

Hardly able to contain his glee at such a happy ending, Mr. Chagla threw his arm around his constable friend.

Dr. Mitra turned to the sergeant. "You haven't charged the prisoner with any crime. Release him into the capable hands of our friend and I will drive them all back to the rest house."

"No, no. Something might happen to him. We are too isolated." I looked to Mr. Chagla for support, but his plump face was stretched in a smile.

"What harm can come to him in our lovely bungalow, sir? We have guards. I am there. Shashi will arrive like a flash if we are in need of help."

"At least let me read the diary. We can collect him tomorrow."

Dr. Mitra objected. "If he stays overnight the police will have to charge him."

Seeing the dismay on Mr. Chagla's face, I accepted defeat and went to Dr. Mitra's car.

The police constables loaded the young man's luggage into the boot. Nitin Bose climbed in beside me, and Dr. Mitra steered the car onto the road.

All the way to the rest house Mr. Chagla chatted happily with Dr. Mitra. His good humor was so much stronger than the silent despair of the young man sitting at my side that I felt almost equal to the situation by the time we reached our gates.

To my relief, Mr. Chagla took immediate charge of our new resident. He bustled about organizing Nitin Bose's luggage and issuing instructions to the cook and to the bearers. Leaving him to show Bose to his rooms, Dr. Mitra and I went to sit on the terrace.

The lights of Mahadeo's temples sparkled reassuringly at the river's bend, and above us Mr. Chagla's round shadow was visible against Nitin Bose's windows as he gesticulated to the bearer serving Bose his dinner.

"Do you think a man can be possessed, Dr. Mitra?" I asked.

"If a man believes strongly enough that he is possessed, then I suppose you could say he is possessed."

"Bose wants to visit a shrine that he thinks can cure him. The local villagers worship there. Will it be all right if he goes with them?"

"Certainly. In fact, I advise it. The young man has imagined his sickness. Let him imagine his cure."

He stood up, seeing Mr. Chagla walking down the garden. "Anyway, let me know what you discover in his diary. It may tell us more about this unfortunate situation."

"Our visitor is tucked up neat and tidy for the night," Mr. Chagla announced with satisfaction as I accompanied him and Dr. Mitra back to the car. "But I have left a guard outside his room, in case he becomes silly again."

As the car's headlights sliced into the darkness of the jungle, I returned to my house to read the young man's diary.

CHAPTER SEVEN

THE EXECUTIVE'S STORY

I suppose in a way my life really began when I came to live on this tea estate. Or perhaps it is ending here.

In any case I know something strange is happening to me, and I must keep a written record of the events leading to my present situation before I am no longer able to relate them.

First I should describe the world I inhabited before I came here. I was a young executive in Calcutta's oldest tea company. Like myself, all my young colleagues had been educated at exclusive boarding schools and obtained their jobs through family connections.

Outside our office Calcutta crumbled under the

weight of neglect, exploitation, poisonous humidity, traffic jams, power failures, and roads plowed up like rice fields to make an underground railway, while a whole generation stoically waited for the city to return to what it once had been as more trainloads of refugees arrived to sleep on railway platforms already overcrowded with refugees from the partition of India fifty years earlier, the war in Bangladesh twenty years earlier, the devastations of nature that daily drew the desperate to a great metropolis itself desperately surviving as if a war had just ended.

But we experienced only claustrophobia as we stared through the darkened windows of our air-conditioned cars at the crowds teeming across the broken pavements.

It was not that we were unfeeling. But we were young and we believed success lay in imitating the anglicized aloofness of our superiors who assured us the city had passed the point of no return.

They counseled us to make the best of a bad job. So we played golf at the Tolleygunge Club. Drank at the Saturday Club. Ate Chinese meals at the Calcutta Club. Raced at the Turf Club.

The drinking helped. And the meaningless adulteries. Also, we read avidly. On our bedside tables the novels of the moment were stacked on top of *Time*, *Newsweek*, the *Economist*, for those nights when there wasn't a woman in the bed. Or for dawn, when we returned from driving our women to their own homes and saw the sheets crumpled with humidity and sweat, saw the long black hairs lying like accusations on the pillow, and knew our lives were leaking away.

Occasionally the sluggish indolence of our lives was disrupted by the arrival of the boys from the tea estates. They were not prematurely aged by their life in the lonely tea gardens like the English tea estate managers described in eighteenth-century diaries, men without teeth or hair who came to Calcutta only to bid for wives when the ships from London discharged their cargoes of desperate Englishwomen trying to escape lives of penury back home.

Our tea garden colleagues were young, good-looking Indians, bursting with alien energy. We listened to their boasts of rogue elephants tracked, man-eating tigers shot, hot-blooded women tamed, and envied the cowboy quality to their headlong pursuit of pleasure during the weeks they spent in the city.

Vying with each other to buy them drinks, we waved at the barman behind the long wooden bar at the Saturday Club. "A patiala peg for the sahib, Moses."

"Come on, yaar, this one's on me."

The tea estate boys obliged us by consuming whole bottles of whisky while we watched, fascinated by their careless self-destruction.

"Yaar, I don't know how your liver can take such punishment."

"Practice, yaar. What do you think I do three hundred and thirty days in the year, up on the estate?"

"What, yaar?"

"Drink, shoot, and fuck."

"Come off it, yaar. Who can you fuck in the wilderness?"

"Armies of women. Real women who will do anything to please a man."

"For instance? No, let me sign for this one."

"Cheers. And what sexual appetites! It's all they think about."

"No wonder you tea estate chaps become such elbow-benders. I couldn't touch those hideous creatures unless I was stinking drunk."

"Come on, yaar, admit it. I bet they smell like hell, your real women."

"I might admit this much. Mrs. Sushila Ghosh smells better than them." The tea estate boy would empty his glass. "And now, yaar. I mustn't keep such a fragrant lady waiting."

Sometimes when I was stuck in a traffic jam behind a bus listing under the weight of passengers clinging to its step rails, I marveled that the clerks squeezed against each other could laugh and joke with each other as they did, and I wondered if the fight for survival could opiate them as luxury had opiated me, or whether they also dreamed of glorious adventures.

And when those free-wheeling tea estate boys came into the office after a night of suicidal drinking followed by lovemaking in air-conditioned bedrooms scented with tuber roses bought fresh every morning from the New Market, I felt a spasm of envious admiration. Life on the tea estates seemed a real man's life.

The nearest we got to danger was gambling. Ashok, who had spent most of his time in the betting shops of London while working toward his accountancy degree, offered odds on the movement of two clouds in the sky outside our office windows. The exact time a peon would take to bring us tea. Whose bored wife's eye would next begin to wander.

Everything was an occasion for a wager. When I was offered the choice between managing a tea estate or going on an executive training course, the betting began again.

"Avoid the estate, yaar. You'll be an alcoholic in a year."

"Six months."

"Nine."

Despite the dire predictions of my companions, I opted for the tea estate.

"Okay, what odds are you giving me? I say it will take him a year."

"Now, Ashok. Don't do all that seven-to-two shit. Just keep it simple. Three to one."

"Done. Three to one says he will be an alcoholic within a year."

"Don't be an ass, yaar Nitin. You will have no one to talk to. Those tea estate buggers are all mad. Driven crazy by loneliness."

To me, suffocated by the sheer weight of Calcutta's inescapable humanity, the solitude of the tea estate was its most attractive prospect.

Still, I found it hard to believe such solitude existed as the jeep wound its way through the deserted Himalayan foothills toward my tea estate.

During the eight-hour drive from the small airport to the tea garden, I stared in awe at the green emptiness stretching in circles below the hill road. Each shepherd beating his animals off the road, each coolie laboring under the bundles tied to his head, required an individual greeting, so rare was human encounter. Overhead the small clouds rose like foam above the distant Himalayas before breaking in a white wave as the wind swept them toward the plains, and I felt like a pebble thrown into a wooded ocean, expanding the empty horizon as an alien object moves the water outward.

Long before I reached my tea estate I had gone from disbelief, to tranquility, to that possessiveness by which one is oneself possessed.

Occasionally the jeep passed a village of thatched cottages that looked more Shakespearean than Indian with their plastered walls and weathered timber beams, isolated in miles of tea bushes just coming into leaf.

As dusk fell we could no longer see the fields of tea bushes. Only the dim lanterns from the tea pickers' colonies broke the darkness. Then night enclosed us in a velvet embrace, and the lights from the tea pickers' huts were no less gentle than the stars in that tranquil sky.

The sweep of our headlights lit the deodar tree spreading its branches above the walls of my new residence. A guard saluted as the jeep rounded a drive outlined by painted bricks, and in the portico five turbanned and cummerbunded servants bowed to me.

It was all so ridiculously English I started laughing. Even when the driver braked and the servants came forward to open my door I could not stop laughing at the thought that I had entered a British fantasy of India, untouched by the chaos of the last forty years.

To reassure the servants that I was as pukka as any other sahib, I began issuing orders in an unnaturally military way. They lost the looks of insecurity brought on by my display of levity, as I supervised the unloading of my luggage. My barked orders, my courtesy underlined by firmness, my eye for detail, drew a portrait of my persona for them to circulate on the estate.

The head bearer ushered me into my bedroom, and I wanted to laugh again when I saw the massive ebony bed with serpents carved on the headboard enclosed in the billowing mosquito net suspended from an iron hoop in the high ceiling, standing there like an altar built for the worship of the senses.

But I controlled myself as the other servants brought in the large cabin trunk my grandfather had taken with him to Cambridge University three years before the Great War. Although he had been a physicist, my grandfather had been an avid reader of Indian philosophy and mythology, and on the day my transfer to the tea gardens had been confirmed my grandmother had sent me his cabin trunk filled with books. I could not imagine why my grandmother thought someone of my generation would have the faintest interest in all those Puranas and Vedas and Upanishads and God knows what. But I had brought them with me in case I ran out of reading material.

Now I ordered the servants to remove the books wedged into the trunk. They looked embarrassed as the volumes piled up on the floor around them. Facing the magnificent bed shrouded in its veils of fine netting was the house's sole bookcase, a plywood construction obviously used by previous inhabitants for pornographic paperbacks or detective stories. A copy of Gorens' *Contract Bridge* lay mournfully on the warping middle shelf.

I instructed the servants to stack the books against the wall until new bookshelves could be made. From the glances they threw in my direction I knew I had succeeded in establishing myself as a scholar, and they would tell the estate workers that I was a just man, capable of controlling my disappointment that my library could not be housed immediately instead of abusing them.

Satisfied by my own performance, I sat alone in the wood-beamed dining room reveling in my good fortune, the only noise the sound of crickets outside and the creaking of the pantry door each time the head bearer brought me another dish.

· · ·

The extraordinary thing about inventing a persona is that one is loathe to give it up, especially if the fiction sits comfortably.

I found I enjoyed being the young paterfamilias of my realm, enjoyed being treated with undisguised respect by the gentle tribal women picking leaves as I walked through the rows of tea bushes with my overseer, Mr. Sen.

A fussy, pedantic man, always looking for the small fault to assert his power, Mr. Sen continually provided me with opportunities to exhibit my tolerant good sense. I took care to do so with a delicacy that could not offend his authority until, over the months, both the tea pickers and the clerical staff under Mr. Sen became dependent on my judgment.

Nature conspired in my fiction that first year. The rains came at exactly the right time to produce the tenderest leaves, and the crop from my estate was the best received by Head Office. The Chairman telegrammed his personal congratulations and the workers responded to their bonus with small presents for me, as if I were a family elder.

I suppose I had begun to exhibit the mannerisms of an elder. Certainly, my old self of the Calcutta days was less and less present, my new self increasingly so, like a shortening shadow merges with its subject. I hardly drank, and I never thought about women. If women showed themselves in my dreams as I lay asleep in the ebony bed, they did so with such subtlety that I awoke with no memory of them.

The dreams I remembered were linked to my grandfather's library.

To my surprise I had become fascinated by the endless legends contained in the Puranas. After a day spent walking through tea gardens laid out with mathematical precision or studying columns of figures at my office desk while the long blades of the wooden fan stirred the air, I found it a delight to sit on the veranda in the evenings reading the labyrinthine tales of demons, sages, gods, lovers, cosmologies.

I even discovered mythological tales dealing with the very area in which my tea estate was situated, legends of a vast underground civilization stretching from these hills all the way to the Arabian Sea, peopled by a mysterious race half human, half serpent. Naturally I viewed the legends through the prism of anthropology, assuming the nomadic Aryan scribes who had recorded the legends had been overwhelmed by the sophistication of the people they had conquered.

But I enjoyed their poetic descriptions of palaces and universities constructed from many-colored marbles. Of gardens more beautiful than those of the gods themselves with ponds of crystalline water alive with leaping fish, silver among the water lilies, and trees bending under the weight of flowering vines. A world devoted to pleasure and learning, its serenity guarded by hooded serpents with great gems flashing from their hoods.

Apparently its inhabitants had even had a particular love of magic, spending happy hours entertaining each other with magic tricks.

After dinner I would sit on the veranda in my wicker armchair, staring into the velvet night, the stars so low in the sky I felt I had only to reach up and pull one down to shed more light on my open book, imagining that the gentle tribals I had seen bending over the tea bushes were in fact descendants of this civilization, still able to do the great Indian rope trick, and when I fell asleep in my ebony bed under the sails of mosquito netting, I dreamed of legendary kingdoms guarded by hooded cobras.

The second year the rains were again kind to us. Our tea crop was so outstanding the Chairman sent a member of the board to invite me to return to Calcutta as a director of the company. To my delight this exalted person turned out to be my friend, Ashok.

"So, yaar, tell me the truth. How long did it take?"

"Did what take?" I asked.

"Be serious, yaar. To become an alcoholic."

He would not believe I was not a drunk until we passed evening after evening on my veranda, I pouring a single drink for myself but many for him. My abstemiousness exasperated him. When I said I did not want to leave the tea estate, Ashok told me I was losing my mind.

Raising his voice above the singing of the crickets and the deep-throated belches of the garden frogs, he said, "You are definitely going mad, yaar. You hardly drink. You want to stay in this god-forsaken wilderness when you could be a director of the company. You mastermind these perfect crops all day but at night you do nothing but read."

He leaned over and stared at me. "Admit it, yaar. It is downright sinister for a man your age not to have had a woman for two solid years!"

He went on and on trying to convince me to return to Calcutta in that soft blackness which had never ceased to affect me as it had from the first night, but which obviously upset him with its emptiness.

Not wishing to offend an old friend, I made excuses. "Which woman would live with me without marriage? And you've seen the tea pickers. Could you take them to bed?"

"Then come back to Calcutta, yaar, before it drops off or withers away like some unwatered tea bush."

Too much drink made him insensitive to my silence, and I was glad the next morning to wave Ashok good-bye.

But his words left a mark on my mind as if he had dropped a bottle of ink across a favorite book. Like some small night animal sexual restlessness began to gnaw at the edges of my content. After dinner I sat on the veranda, unable to relax in the wicker armchair as insects and moths flung themselves ceaselessly against the glass domes covering the lightbulbs. The darkness that had always seemed so serene now mirrored my restless mind. For the first time I was lonely, and when I entered my bedroom I felt the massive bed sneering at my unused manhood.

Whatever I saw mocked my efforts to recover my composure. The women laughing at each other across the tea bushes now seemed knowingly voluptuous, revealing their breasts, their rounded bellies, their bared calves too much to my view. Even when I went shooting in the jungle I heard only the mating call of animals and I was disgusted with the gun in my hands.

My grandfather's books offered no escape. Once I pulled the Rig Veda from the bookshelf, hoping to find some philosophical consolation in it, but the passage I read shocked me, so accurately did it describe my loneliness.

At first was Death.
That which did mean an utter emptiness.
And emptiness, mark thou, is Hunger's Self.

Determined to recover my tranquility, I plunged into my work with redoubled intensity. It did no good. Everything about my work annoyed me. The stupidity of the workers with their constant demands for advances against their salaries. The stubbornness of the union leaders. The inefficiency of the clerical staff in the office.

I frequently found myself shouting in irritation when something small had been overlooked, as if I had become Mr. Sen. The workers responded by withdrawing their affection, leaving me frozen in that isolation which had led so many of my colleagues to become alcoholics.

Now I followed the example of my predecessors, putting aside my books to sit in the darkness, a bottle of whisky at my elbow, while the head bearer waited in the garden, drawing on his bidi as I drank myself into oblivion. Then, my body a dead weight across his shoulders, he dragged me into the bedroom and somehow undressed me and pushed me through the mosquito net where I lay in a stupor of stale whisky fumes never sure if I was awake or asleep.

Perhaps my loneliness caused my mind to create its own enslavement. Or perhaps I had already become the victim of my grandfather's books. In any case, one night I was lying in my bed when I was awakened by a perfume that subsumed the smell of whisky that had become the companion to my sleep.

As that musky fragrance enveloped me, calming me and exciting me at the same time, I felt a softness press against my shoulder. Stretching out my hand, I grasped the swelling firmness of a woman's breast. But the petals of a flower garland intruded between my lips and her flesh, a girdle chain between my thigh and her smooth hip, an anklet between my hand and her slender foot. Maddened by the fragile barrier of her ornaments, I crushed her in my embrace. Her body encircled mine like a flowering creeper grips a tree. She made a sound between a sigh and a laugh, her breath moist against my ear. Then a low voice asked, "Why did you not send for me earlier?"

Was I bewitched that night by the moon throwing its feverish light across the bed, gilding her supple body silver as she rode mine? Or was it the long eyes sliding like fish above her slanting Mongol cheekbones? The slender shoulders pulled forward by the weight of her breasts? The perspiration shining on her narrow waist above the mango curve of her hip?

Was it the perfect oval cast by our shadow on the sheets as she pressed her feet against my chest when I enclosed her in my embrace? The sight of her limbs turning the dark blue of a lotus calyx as the clouds obscured the moon? Or was it the heavy plait coiling and uncoiling against our bodies until it unraveled under the billowing curtain of the mosquito net to cocoon us in a second curtain, blacker than the night outside?

I did not know whether I had fashioned her from the night and my own hunger, even though her small teeth pierced my skin again and again like the sudden striking of a snake, and I heard the hissing of her pleasure against my throat. But when she left my bed I was already asleep, dreaming I still held a creature half serpent in my arms, my sated senses pulling me into the underground world of my grandfather's legends.

If in the morning the mirror had not reflected the vermilion marks of her painted feet on my chest or the streaks of her black collyrium on my skin I would not have believed she existed. Seeing them, I was sick with love as if I had been pierced by all five arrows of desire.

The next night I lay in my bed, my limbs trembling in anticipation as I waited for her. Yet I was asleep again when her low voice in my ear awoke me, and I was again asleep before she left me.

Knowing the urgency of my desire, I could not understand my inability to stay awake. After the first few nights I realized I was enchanted.

What can I tell you of the months that followed? I was intoxicated by a pleasure that left me both satisfied and delicately unsatisfied. I never saw her by daylight, and if I had I would not have recognized her. At some point in our lovemaking she had revealed her name was Rima, yet I did not search for her among the tribal women bending over the tea bushes, fearful that the brilliant sun might rob me of my enchantment.

My body knew the contours of her body, my hands the features of her face, but to my eyes she was an endless play of shadows, entering my bed in darkness when I was no longer capable of waiting for her so that always she surprised my senses.

She even knew when when our passion was in danger of becoming repetition. Then she seduced me with tribal songs in a language I could not understand so that I heard only the sweetness of the melodies. She told me tales of a great serpent kingdom lying inches beneath the soil. She spoke to me of charms that gave men the strength of elephants in rut and of magic performed during the eclipse of the moon when a man's soul could be captured inside the two halves of a coconut.

She swore she had seen an old woman raise flames from the palms of her hands, and a tribal priest cover a mango seedling with his shawl, then pull it away to reveal a dwarf tree bending under the weight of ripe mangoes. Swarming like clusters of black bees in the whiteness of her eyes, her pupils mesmerized me as her low voice gave substance to the worlds I had dreamed of when reading my grandfather's books.

Once again I took pleasure in my work as manager of the garden, and the tea pickers again treated me with the esteem they had withdrawn. Maybe they laughed at me when I sometimes did not answer their questions, but often the only sound I heard were her songs floating in my mind.

For a long time I believed these melodic fragments surfaced from my unconscious. When I finally realized they were actually being sung by the women as they picked leaves, I asked Mr. Sen to translate the words.

Poor Mr. Sen looked embarrassed but at my insistence he mournfully translated,

"Which god is notorious
  In the neighborhood?

"Look! It is the god of fucking
  Who is notorious in the neighborhood."

The women noticed what we were doing and shouted with laughter as they changed their song.

"On the hill
  See the peacock's feathers sway
  As I am swaying on your lap,
  Sighing on your lap,
  Smiling on your lap.
  O, my handsome friend."

Then to my delight the women began singing the song Rima often sang to awaken me, and I wrote the words down as Mr. Sen translated.

"Bring me my oil and my collyrium.
  Sister, bring my mirror and the vermilion.
  Make haste with my flower garland.
  My lover waits impatient in the bed."

For a year Rima came to me every night, sliding into my ebony bed to coil her limbs around me.

Like a magician she drew me into a subterranean world of dream, her body teaching mine the passing of the seasons, the secret rhythms of nature, until I understood why my grandfather's books called these hills Kamarupa, the Kingdom of the God of Love.

The Chairman's telegram ended my delirium. "Head Office reorganizing Company. Proceed to Calcutta immediately to study innovations."

I tore the telegram in a rage, certain that Ashok had forced the Chairman's decision, but there was nothing I could do. The telegram was not a suggestion. It was a command.

Rima wept as if her heart were breaking when I told her I was leaving. Gratified by her tears, I made love to her with an ardor that surprised me, so exhausted by my exertions I almost didn't hear her ask "Should I return to my husband? He works as a coolie at the railway depot in Agartala. Should I join him while you are gone?"

Such was my enchantment with Rima's strangeness that I did not find it odd that she was married. And I could tolerate the thought that another man might embrace her. After all, who had I slept with all those years in Calcutta but other men's wives?

But that he should be a coolie. That I should

love a coolie's wife. Waves of disgust engulfed me and I wanted to vomit with shame. At that moment the spell in which Rima held me was broken. For the first time I remained awake when she climbed out of the bed to wrap herself in her sarong. Her limbs were squat and ugly in the light of dawn.

How glad I was to return to Calcutta and the insouciance of my old life of clubs, friends, and betting.

The very superficiality of my colleagues dulled my shame. How hard I laughed at their jokes as they bought drinks for me at the bars of the Saturday Club, the Tolleygunge Club, the Calcutta Club, the Turf Club.

How lightheartedly I flirted with the sophisticated, husky-voiced women whose boredom I briefly diverted by the novelty of my presence. And when they took me to their bedrooms, I kept the lights on as I kissed their large eyes that did not slant upward like Rima's, until I buried the memory of Rima's body in their warm brown flesh.

I could no longer resist the excitement of Head Office. The international shipping arrangements and insurance problems, the constant deadlines presented by bids taken in London or Hong Kong, made my life in the tea garden seem primitive, governed as it was by the grinding slowness of the changing seasons. I did not want to go back to that isolated house or the demands of the bovine tea pickers. I did not want to return to Rima.

Encouraged by Ashok, the Chairman invited me again to become a director. This time I accepted eagerly and it was agreed that I would return to the tea garden to organize things for my successor, then take a few weeks' leave before assuming my new appointment.

I felt a certain trepidation at returning to the tea estate for the last time. Rima had wept so much at my departure for Calcutta that I dreaded her reaction when she learned I would be leaving her permanently.

I could no longer remember any desire for Rima but I could not overlook her poverty, and I decided it was only fair that she should earn something from our association. Hoping to avoid recriminations, I left money with the head bearer, instructing him to deliver it to Rima.

To my surprise she did not try to see me. I knew she was in the tea garden because at night I heard a voice singing in the darkness outside,

"Bring me my oil and my collyrium.
Sister, bring me my mirror and the vermilion."

I pretended not to hear and continued reading, but even in my cowardice I appreciated Rima's discretion in leaving me alone, which seemed so elegant in someone of her origins.

Her subtlety was greater than I understood. By standing outside my bedroom every night, she succeeded in turning my cowardice into guilt. Night after night I lay in the ebony bed unable to concentrate on my book as I listened to the voice outside my window singing,

"Make haste with my flower garland.
My lover waits impatient in the bed."

Unable to tolerate my guilt, one night I opened the door leading into the garden. I could still hear her singing but there was no one there. Then I heard her call, "Nitin. Nitin Bose."

"Rima, come inside. I want to talk to you." There was no answer so I repeated my request. Again she did not respond. For several minutes I stood there calling her to come inside, but no one replied.

Instead of returning to my room, I waited in the shadows. After a while I heard a rustling in the undergrowth, then the sound of breaking twigs as footsteps retreated into the woods that ringed my house. I ran to the wall. As I flung my leg over it I heard her call again, "Nitin. Nitin Bose."

"Rima, wait! I must talk to you!" I shouted.

"Nitin Bose!" The voice grew fainter as she ran into the trees. The darkness was so dense I wished I had taken a torch from the guard so I could see my way. Then I remembered the moon was in eclipse that night, and the superstitious guard would not venture out of doors on a night so full of ill omen.

Heedless of the low branches whipping against my body, I ran after her through the jungle, calling her name, my voice loud in the night.

Suddenly, almost in front of me, she shouted, "Nitin. Nitin Bose."

"Yes," I answered in surprise. There was the noise of something being clapped over something else, like two books slapped together. As I heard that sound I felt the air being sucked out of my lungs.

Nothing touched me but I felt as if a pump had been forcibly placed over my lips and nose. I gasped for air, unable to breathe. Over the noise of my own suffocation I heard laughter, then the striking of a match. A lantern flared in the darkness, lighting a woman's face from below as she adjusted the flame.

Rima placed the lantern at her feet and retrieved something from the ground.

"You will never leave me now, no matter how far you go," she said triumphantly, waving her trophy in front of me. It was a coconut, the split halves covering each other. I clutched at her, feeling myself begin to fall, but she eluded me and I hit the ground. Picking up her lantern, she disappeared into the jungle.

I lay under the trees, the stench of decomposing vegetation filling my nostrils as I tried to suck air into my bursting lungs. Over my harsh breathing I could hear her vengeful song growing fainter and fainter in the darkness:

"Bring me my oil and my collyrium.
Sister, bring my mirror and the vermilion.
Make haste with my flower garland.
My lover waits impatient in the bed."

It is the last clear memory I have.

The passage that follows was dictated by the head bearer at my request.

"At dawn the guard made a round of the house before he went to his quarters. The door of your bedroom was open and your bed had not been slept in. Finding you nowhere on the grounds, the guard went to search for you in the woods.

"He found you lying in the mud. He asked if you were all right but you talked only nonsense, calling the name Rima again and again and singing a song our tribal women sing at the time of marriage.

"The guard ran to my room and woke me up. Together we managed to carry you from the woods to your bed. We could see you were not physically ill and we were frightened. We realized you had gone out during the eclipse. Perhaps you did not know that a man can become fatally ill or mad if he walks outside during the eclipse of the moon. We sent for the priest of the tribal village to ask his advice before we informed Mr. Sen.

"The priest tried to talk to you, asking why you had been walking in the jungle on such an inauspicious night. Who had you gone to meet. But you just sang and called this Rima's name, your eyes so strange, like a madman's. The priest told us to let no one see you and he went away.

"He returned an hour later with a covered basket. He asked me to heat some milk while he went to your bedside. I brought the warm milk, thinking he had some medicine for you. When I reached your bed I screamed with fear and dropped it. The priest was holding a snake only inches from your face and reciting some spell. I could see the snake's tongue flicking out to touch the skin of your face. But you did not wince, or even blink. That frightened me even more.

"I heated fresh milk. The priest took the bowl and put it on the floor for the snake. While the snake was drinking the milk he prayed to it in a language I could not understand. Suddenly you said to him, 'What are you doing in my room?'

"The priest explained you had been singing and talking about a woman named Rima. He asked you to get up and write an account of everything you remembered about your association with her.

"All day you sat at your desk writing. The effort exhausted you and you were already asleep when the priest returned. He asked me to warm some milk and performed the same ceremony of the morning, praying to the snake while it drank the milk. At that point you woke up, but you were not strange-seeming any more. You even told the priest, 'I don't know what made me behave this way.'

"The priest explained, 'Someone has taken possession of you. The magic you are under is stronger than my powers. It will start exerting its strength again. Your memory will be affected. You will believe yourself to be someone else.'

" 'What nonsense!' you shouted at the priest. 'I

don't believe in magic. Someone must be trying to poison me. Was I bitten by that snake?'

" 'This serpent has helped you. But only a little. And not for very long.'

"You refused to believe the priest. For the next week you sent for the doctor every day. The doctor kept telling you there was nothing wrong with you. Then you began drinking whisky, but the more you drank the less control you had over your mind, singing that song about oil and vermilion or calling yourself Rima. Finally I sent for the priest again.

"He told me, 'If your sahib wants to recover his mind he must worship the goddess at any shrine that overlooks the Narmada River. Only that river has been given the power to cure him.' "

CHAPTER EIGHT

When I finally closed Nitin Bose's diary, it was too late to sleep. I was sorry for the young man, but his story made no sense to me. Exhausted by my own incomprehension, I went to the terrace.

As always, the darkness that precedes the dawn stilled my mind. I could not see the Narmada, but I sat with my face turned to the east where the river reveals herself to the holy men ringing the pool at Amarkantak, wondering what the ascetics thought about as they watched the water flowing from some secret stream, whispering in eddies below their crossed legs, mysterious and alluring in the dying night.

Did they brood on the Narmada as the proof of Shiva's great penance, or did they imagine her as a beautiful woman dancing toward the Arabian Sea, arousing the lust of ascetics like themselves while Shiva laughed at the madness of their infatuation?

Dawn lightened the sky and I was able to see the Narmada leaping headlong through the distant marble rocks, the spraying waterfalls refracting the first rays of sun into arcs of color as if the river were a woman adorning herself with jewels.

Below the terrace the water was still dark, appearing motionless in the shadows like a woman indolently stretching her limbs as she oiled herself with scented oils, her long black hair loosened, her eyes outlined in collyrium.

I watched the water slowly redden, catching reflections from the rose colors of dawn, and imagined the river as a woman painting her palms and the soles of her feet with vermilion as she prepared to meet her lover.

It was the first time I had entertained such thoughts about the river. Now the legends of the Narmada merged with Nitin Bose's story as I struggled to understand the power of the woman who had enchanted him.

If even the Great Ascetic could not withstand the weapons unleashed from Kama's sugarcane bow strung with honeybees, how could poor Nitin

Bose survive as Kama's arrows found their mark, piercing him with enchantment, inflaming him with lust, parching him with desire, rendering him helpless with the paroxysms of his own longing, until he was wounded with that fifth and fatal arrow, the Carrier of Death?

The sun appeared above the Vindhya Hills, a fiery ball of light leeching the color from the water until it shone like glass, as hard as woman's pursuit of a lover. The bright light hurt my eyes. I turned from the terrace and saw the staff waiting for my instructions. I issued the first orders of the morning. Then I wrote a note to Mr. Chagla advising him to keep an eye on Nitin Bose because I was going to bed.

"Sir! Wake up, sir. You must get ready!"

I opened my eyes. Mr. Chagla's round face was peering down at me, moisture beading his fingerprints on an iced glass.

"Here, sir. Drink some juice."

"How is our visitor, Chagla?"

"Excellent, sir. You will see when he comes back from the shrine."

"You let him go to the shrine by himself?"

"As if, sir! The guards went with him. Also, their wives."

"They are illiterate villagers." I could hear my

voice rising with fear. "Why didn't you accompany him? What if he harms himself?"

"I couldn't, sir. They will not let outsiders come to their shrine. But I have given stern instructions. Mr. Bose must be returned to us in A-one condition."

"How has Bose gone with them? He is not a tribal."

"They say he has been touched by the power of the goddess so he is not an outsider any more. Anyway, don't perturb youself, sir. I know everything what is going to happen. Their shrine is only a big banyan tree. Nothing harmful. There the villagers will have an assembly with Mr. Bose. Now hurry, sir. You must take refreshment. The cook is waiting in the dining room with your meal."

Mr. Chagla left my room and I washed hastily. As I was dressing I shouted to him through the closed door, "What happens in the assembly? Did the guards tell you?"

"The tribals will beg the goddess to forgive Mr. Bose for denying the power of desire."

"Power of desire?" I demanded as I came out, reassured by the brilliant afternoon sunlight and my starched clothes. "Chagla, have you been infected by this foolishness?"

Mr. Chagla looked at me with the anxiety of a

parent watching a willful child. "But, sir, without desire there is no life. Everything will stand still. Become emptiness. In fact sir, be dead."

I stared at him in astonishment, and Mr. Chagla's smooth face wrinkled with the effort of making me comprehend. "It is not a woman who has taken possession of Mr. Bose's soul, sir. How can such a thing can ever happen?"

"Then what is all this goddess business?"

"Sir. Really, sir." Mr. Chagla sighed in frustration. "The goddess is just the principle of life. She is every illusion that is inspiring love. That is why she is greater than all the gods combined. Call her what you will, but she is what a mother is feeling for a child. A man for a woman. A starving man for food. Human beings for God. And Mr. Bose did not show her respect so he is being punished."

"By sitting under a tree?"

"No sir. He will not be sitting. The villagers will be sitting. Mr. Bose will be making a mud image of the goddess."

"What for?"

"To carry to the river for immersing purposes. I have found a spot where we can observe the procession, hidden from the human eye. But you must eat first, sir. These tribals have no sense of time."

I could feel the situation sliding out of my control. "What is the point of the procession?"

"Ritual, ritual, and ritual, sir. Like repeating your two-times table."

"Chagla, you are not making sense."

"Certainly I am, sir. It is Mr. Bose who is making no sense, pretending desire is some kind of magic performed with black arts. But desire is the origin of life. For thousands of years our tribals have worshipped it as the goddess. You have heard the pilgrims praying 'Save us from the serpent's venom.' Well, sir, the meaning of the prayer is as follows. The serpent in question is desire. Its venom is the harm a man does when he is ignoring the power of desire."

Defeated by Mr. Chagla's good nature, I walked to the dining room, wondering if his open face and rotund body hid an understanding that I did not possess. As I ate, I tried to fathom what Mr. Chagla had been saying while my eyes wandered idly over the mosaics of flowers and birds inlaid into the dining-room walls.

The sound of drumbeats and singing voices brought Mr. Chagla running into the room. "Sir, hurry! The procession is coming through the jungle."

I ran up the stairs followed by the cook and

other curious members of the bungalow staff. We crowded onto the terrace of Nitin Bose's suite, which overlooked the jungle.

Trees obscured the steep path leading down to the riverbank, but there was an open space where we could see a line of villagers following a garlanded idol carried on a platform supported by long bamboo poles. Four men held the poles to their shoulders. I recognized them as bungalow guards. Behind them I caught a brief glimpse of Nitin Bose's face. Then he disappeared down the curve of the path, and I could see only the idol above the bushes, rocking on its platform as the men descended the steep incline.

Mr. Chagla gently pulled at my elbow, whispering conspiratorially "Sir, let us go to my hidey-hole to observe the ceremony."

I followed him down the stairs and into the garden. At a corner of the garden he opened a rusting iron gate that led to the water tanks below the terrace. The path was used once a year when the water tanks were inspected. Now Mr. Chagla walked in front of me crushing nettles and weeds underfoot to clear the way to a rock escarpment halfway down the hillside.

We crouched behind a boulder as the procession skidded down the steep path. Mr. Chagla had chosen a perfect vantage point. We had a clear view of the riverbank two hundred feet below us, and I could even see fish swimming in the clear water of the river slowly turning gray in the approaching dusk.

The procession stumbled down the slope, and the guards yelled to each other, struggling to keep the idol from sliding off the tilting platform as they lowered it to the ground.

The procession of villagers fell back to allow Nitin Bose to approach the idol. He looked dazed. For a long moment he stood in front of the mud image and nothing happened. Then, as if he had suddenly remembered an instruction, he put his arms around the idol, lifting it from the ground. Holding the idol, he walked into the water. The tribals waded in behind him, their hands raised, their faces turned to the west. The crimson sunset reddened their features as Nitin Bose immersed the idol in the river, chanting

"Salutations in the morning and at night to thee, O Narmada.
Defend me from the serpent's poison."

The mud idol began to disintegrate in the current, and we watched fragments of the image being swept downstream—a broken arm, a breast, torn garlands spinning in the water as they were carried toward the clay lamps floating in the darkness at the river's bend.

The temple bells from Mahadeo were ringing for the evening prayers. Mr. Chagla got to his feet and began stamping down the nettles. "It will be completely dark soon, sir. Let us return to the bungalow before we are eaten up by snakes."

I stood up. Below us I could barely see the shadowy figures of the Vano villagers still standing around Bose in the water. I followed Mr. Chagla up the pathway to the bungalow, the voices of the villagers growing fainter as they chanted after Nitin Bose,

"Salutations in the morning and at night to thee, O Narmada.
Defend me from the serpent's poison."

For three weeks Nitin Bose remained in the bungalow, a source of constant concern to me.

I could not concentrate on my dawn meditations listening to him sliding down the steep path that led to the river. I was always afraid he would fall or be bitten by a snake before he reached the riverbank to make his salutation.

In the evenings I no longer enjoyed watching the sunset from our terrace for fear some harm might come to him standing waist deep in the water below me, praying to the Narmada.

Never having been a parent, I found this unfamiliar burden of responsibility an irritant. I considered Nitin Bose a foolish young man who attracted misfortune, even though Mr. Chagla told me he appeared to be working on something because his desk was covered with papers.

I was greatly relieved when Nitin Bose finally left us and the bungalow returned to its routine serenity.

Shortly after his departure I received a letter from my old colleague thanking me for looking after his nephew.

"I knew I could rely on your discretion. Incidentally, Nitin showed me a most interesting essay he has written concerning the tribal practices in your area. I have asked him to submit it to the *Asia Review* for publication."

Mr. Chagla was pleased to hear about the essay. "And guess what, sir?"

"What, Chagla?"

"Only yesterday I heard some village children

singing on the path to Vano. Do you know what they were singing?

" *'Bring me my oil and my collyrium.*
Sister, bring my mirror and the vermilion.'

"Nothing is ever lost, sir. That is the beauty of a river view."

CHAPTER NINE

Dr. Mitra had been away in Delhi attending a medical conference. Now we were sitting on the wide veranda of the bungalow having tea while I brought him up to date with Nitin Bose's story.

It was late afternoon and the sultry atmosphere that precedes the monsoons seemed to be lifting at last. A light breeze was blowing in from the river, bringing hope of rain.

"An interesting case," Dr. Mitra observed as I ended my account. "But probably not unusual."

A sudden bark of laughter shook the lanky frame on which the white cotton shirt and trousers seemed to flap as if suspended on a hanger. "Someone is sure to commemorate Nitin Bose's recovery by building a temple where he immersed the idol. It will become a place of pilgrimage, attracting hosts of lunatics to your riverbank."

"Have you ever had patients who claimed to be possessed?" I asked, unable to imagine anyone sharing Nitin Bose's ailment.

"Not possessed exactly, but pulled in two directions. Only to be expected when we are sitting on the battleground between the Aryans and the pre-Aryans."

I idly watched a fallen blossom roll across the grass below the veranda. "What does that have to do with being possessed?"

"My dear fellow. This is where the war for the possession of India was fought—pitting Aryan reason against the primal beliefs of the tribals. Though they weren't tribals at all, really. As Nitin Bose noted in his diary, they had a civilization long before the Aryans arrived, with great cities and so forth. Called themselves Nagas and worshipped the Naga, the snake. In my opinion the Sanskrit word for city, nagara, comes from them."

He stretched out his long legs and leaned back into the cushions of the cane armchair, narrowing his eyes against the afternoon sun slanting across the river. "Did you know 'narmada' means 'whore' in Sanskrit?"

I was offended. "That's impossible. The Narmada is the holiest river in India."

He turned toward me, his lean face creased with amusement. "Ah, yes. I forgot. A mere glimpse of the Narmada's waters is supposed to cleanse a human being of generations of sinful births. Just think how pure you and I must be, gazing on this river every day."

I ignored Dr. Mitra's sarcasm. "So Narmada is unlikely to mean whore."

He shook a bony forefinger at me. "I hope you are not contracting the fatal Indian disease of making everything holy, my friend. The Narmada is already too holy by half. Do you know how many sacred spots there are supposed to be on her banks? Four hundred billion, according to the Puranic scriptures."

I didn't argue. Dr. Mitra is something of a scholar on the Narmada, part of the general eccentricity of his nature that has led him to run a six-bed hospital in the small town of Rudra in preference to the lucrative practice that his many medical degrees could have gained him in any of our large cities. He maintains that he encounters more interesting patients here than he could hope to find in Delhi or Bombay, and whenever he describes a pilgrim brought to him with only one-third of a body or some particularly horrifying form of elephantiasis, his eyes shine with excitement as if he is describing a work of art.

It is odd that someone as skeptical as Dr. Mitra should enjoy the stories of the river, but his wayward temperament seems to delight in unraveling the threads of mythology, archaeology, anthropology in which the river is entangled.

As if reading my thoughts Dr. Mitra said, "You know, the great Alexandrine geographer Ptolemy wrote about the Narmada. I suppose even the Greeks and the Alexandrines had heard about the Narmada's holiness and the religious suicides at Amarkantak—people fasting to death or immolating themselves on the Narmada's banks, or drowning in her waters—in order to gain release from the cycle of birth and rebirth."

He shook his head in disbelief at the extremes to which religious folly could take men.

"The ancient Greeks would probably have sympathized with the river's mythology, but at least they had to deal with only one set of myths, whereas Indians have never been prepared to settle for a single mythology if they could squeeze another hundred in."

I laughed at Dr. Mitra's expression of incomprehension as he expanded on the excesses of the devout.

"On top of all that mythology, there's the river's astrology. Her holiness is believed to dispel the malevolent effects of Saturn so all manner of epileptics, depressives, and other unfortunates rush to her banks. And yet, the Narmada is also a magnet to scholars. Towns on the banks of the river are renowned for the learning of their Brahmins. It is as if reason and instinct are constantly warring on the banks of the Narmada. I mean, even the war between the Aryans and the pre-Aryans is still unresolved here."

"After four thousand years?"

"My dear chap. What about the temple of Supaneshwara on the north bank of the Narmada?"

I reluctantly admitted that I had never heard of it.

"But you must have heard of the Immortal who sleeps in the forests near the temple."

"What is an Immortal?" I asked, faintly irritated by Dr. Mitra's heavy-handed display of mystery.

"An Aryan warrior."

"Are you telling me that a four-thousand-year-old Aryan warrior is asleep on the north bank of the Narmada?"

"Absolutely, my dear fellow." Dr. Mitra gave me a gleeful smile. "I can even tell you his name. Avatihuma."

"I've never heard such nonsense in all my life."

"Ask any local tribal. Your guard is from Vano. He'll corroborate my story."

I couldn't resist the challenge and shouted for Mr. Chagla. A round head appeared through the office window, happily nodding assent when I asked for the guard.

Dr. Mitra tapped my arm. "Now remember, the pre-Aryans had lived here peacefully for centuries, perhaps even millennia, before the Aryans arrived. Their philosophy was based on a profound respect for nature and the interdependence of all life.

"Then along came the Aryans. Restless nomads. Obsessed with conquest. Reveling in war. Placing the truths learned by the mind above all other truths, including the truths of nature. In other words, the war between the pre-Aryans and the Aryans was a classic conflict between instinct and reason. Rather like the conflict that drove Nitin Bose mad. In any case, the pre-Aryans slaughtered a number of Aryans. But the Aryan warriors had been granted immortality by their gods. And immortals cannot die. Ah, here's the guard."

A tall man in a khaki uniform was standing on the grass below the veranda, a stout bamboo stave held in one hand. With the other hand he saluted. Dr. Mitra clasped his own hands together in greeting before asking "Have you ever heard of a temple called Supaneshwara?"

"Yes, sahib. My father went on a pilgrimage there."

"Is it easy to find?"

The guard looked dubious. "It's not far from here. But the jungle is very thick in those hills where the river rises, sahib."

"I wonder if I could go there . . ." Dr. Mitra was only thinking aloud, but the guard became quite agitated at his words.

"Don't, sahib. My father nearly lost his life on the journey. Bandits and all sorts of bad elements live in those parts. There are no villages to provide shelter to the traveler so anyone can strike at will."

I was curious to know why the area had so many bandits. "Can't the police catch them?"

"Impossible. A man can disappear forever in such jungles. But that is not the only reason bandits go there, sahib. They also seek the Immortal."

"Who is this Immortal?" I asked with growing impatience.

"Of the race who conquered my people. Even though my ancestors severed his head from his body, he could not be killed. To this day the head just lies in the jungle, sahib. Sleeping because it cannot die."

Dr. Mitra's curiosity won over his triumph at proving me wrong. "What do the bandits do when they find it?"

"Honeybees are said to circle the Immortal's head, sahib. The bandits believe if they are stung by one of the honeybees, they cannot be killed in a police shootout."

Dr. Mitra stretched full length in his chair, grinning with pleasure at having learned yet another tale to add to the tales that seem to multiply around this astonishing river.

There was the deep rumble of thunder and the sun was suddenly obscured by scudding storm clouds. The guard walked back to his post lifting his face to the raindrops falling intermittently from the darkening sky. Then jagged lightning ripped open the black clouds, deluging the garden in the first storm of the monsoon.

Mr. Chagla hurried onto the veranda and began lowering the rolled cane screens tied between the pillars. The heavy downpour roused Dr. Mitra from his reverie. "I'd better give you a lift back to town, Chagla. The road will be slush in a few minutes."

Mr. Chagla accepted with alacrity. I could tell from the uncharacteristic glumness of his expression that he was already dreading the weeks ahead when he would have to cycle on flooded mud paths through the monsoon storms to get to work.

Over the next month I had no time to think of bandits.

Even during a light monsoon the steep hill be-hind the bungalow traps the rain, sending torrents of muddy water down the hillside to inundate our grounds. Broken branches fall on the single elec-tric line that connects us to the power station at Rudra, and the bungalow generator is so old it cannot cope with our frequent power failures. Poor Mr. Chagla is continually loading spare parts for the generator into a hired three-wheeler at Rudra and navigating his way through the deep puddles left in the mud path by bullock-cart wheels to restore the bungalow's power supply.

Fortunately we never have visitors during these months and are able to see to the bungalow's maintenance without unnecessary distraction.

This year the monsoon was unexpectedly heavy and the generator had hardly worked at all, al-though Mr. Chagla had practically rebuilt it in order to run our lights.

One morning I was sitting behind my desk in the office, unable to work. With nothing to stir the air, the humidity was already making my clothes stick to my skin. I stared at the black rainclouds darkening the sky outside, resenting this season when the driving rain keeps me imprisoned indoors, and waited impatiently for Mr. Chagla to arrive and work some miracle on the generator.

At last the three-wheeler backfired at the gates and Mr. Chagla's oval form crossed the garden. Mud stained his trousers to the knees but his head was obscured by his large black umbrella, so it was only when he turned toward the house that I saw the elderly woman sheltering under his arm.

"Can we keep a visitor, sir?" Mr. Chagla asked as he entered my office, morosely shaking the leg of his sodden trousers.

"In the middle of the monsoons? Impossible, Chagla. Nothing is working."

"Even only for a night or two?"

"Chagla, be reasonable. We are not prepared for a guest."

"But the road is practically submerged, sir. My three-wheeler stalled. Water flooded the engine. Everything was a complete flop. Then I saw this lady walking on the road. She told me she was on her way to a temple north of here. I asked her to help me push the three-wheeler but, poor thing, she was too frail to do anything. She looked so fatigued, as if she were going to drop any moment. I couldn't just leave her there, sir."

"Where is she now, Chagla?" I asked in exasperation.

"In the drawing room."

"I'd better warn her that she is not going to be very comfortable."

The smell of damp upholstery overwhelmed me as I entered the high-ceilinged chamber built to keep cool in the worst heat of summer. Now the small windows threw the room into heavy shadow so that only the colors of the butterflies and flowers that adorned the marble mosaics glowed. The woman was standing in the middle of the room staring at the mosaics. She turned at my approach, and in that shadowy light it took me a moment to see that her mud-spattered sari was white.

"How long do you want to stay here?" I asked ungraciously.

"Just tonight, sir." Her face was so thin the lines that creased her skin were more prominent than her features. "Tomorrow I will come back with my daughter to collect my belongings."

A radiant smile suddenly brightened her expression and I realized she must have once been beautiful. "Then, sir, I will take my daughter home at last."

"Has your daughter run away?" I am always

reluctant to allow the bungalow to become the battleground for a family dispute.

"Oh, sir, if only God had been so kind." She began weeping and I hastily changed the subject.

"Where is your daughter at the moment?"

"Near a temple called Supaneshwara. I looked on the map. It must be quite close."

I did not remember where I had heard of the temple or I might have been able to prevent a tragedy. But I was only concerned to stop the woman's weeping. Her next words aroused my suspicions again. "I pray my daughter will not be scarred forever by her experience."

"Experience, madam?"

"Oh, sir, my daughter was kidnapped two years ago."

"Good God. We must inform the police immediately."

I turned to leave the room. The woman clutched my arm. "No. You will put her life in jeopardy. The police gave up the search months ago. They are afraid of my daughter's captors. I was there when she was kidnapped. I saw the men who stole my daughter. If you had seen their faces, you would know there is no cruelty of which they are incapable."

She sagged, her weight dragging me down. I put my hand under her elbow and led her to a chair.

At that moment Mr. Chagla entered the room with a tea tray. He solicitously poured a cup of tea for our distressed visitor, and she wiped her tears with the edge of her sari before sipping from her cup.

I thought the tea had calmed her, but when she spoke again it was clear she still feared I would inform the police.

"I have lost my child once, sir. I beg you, do not endanger her life again. Let me tell you how my daughter was stolen from me. Then you will understand why the police have abandoned her."

CHAPTER TEN

THE COURTESAN'S STORY

Fifty years ago, in the days when there were still kingdoms in India, our small state of Shahbag was famed throughout India for its culture.

Too small to be of interest to the British Empire, perhaps Shahbag was saved by its size. Our ruler, the Nawab of Shahbag, was awarded no British gun salutes and the viceroy never visited. But if we were denied imperial splendor, in our isolation we were able to maintain the truer splendor of civilized behavior.

It was easy to cultivate civility in the beauty of our setting. You see, 'Shahbag' means 'garden of the emperor.' Our capital gained its name from the Emperor Jehangir's pleasure when he saw the fields of flowers growing on our riverbank and, beyond, the Narmada stretching twelve miles across, as wide as an ocean.

Once a year, as schoolchildren, we joined our ruler in showering blossoms on its waters. The Nawab was a Muslim but he honored the river's holiness. I can still hear his voice echoing through the microphones: "Bathing in the waters of the Jamuna purifies a man in seven days, in the waters of the Saraswati in three, in the waters of the Ganges in one, but the Narmada purifies with a single sight of her waters. Salutations to thee, O Narmada."

Then we all shouted "Salutations to thee, O Narmada!" and flung our garlands into the water, competing to throw them farthest.

In those days if you went for a boat ride you could see people promenading in the gardens that stretched the entire length of the city or lying by the flower beds that led to the water's edge, and in the evenings there were always musicians playing in the wind pavilions. Then, as night fell, above the gardens you could watch the skyline of the city being etched into the darkness as lamps were lit in the mosques, the arched balconies of the Nawab's palace, the windows of the grand houses of the aristocrats. Our haveli was one of the grand houses. The less wealthy lived on streets leading to some central point, a bazaar or a place of worship, so that the whole city had a symmetry that pleased the eye.

Wide boulevards bordered the river gardens. Now the globed gas lamps imported from Paris by the Nawab have all been removed, but when I was a child their light cast a romantic glow over the horse-drawn carriages in which the gentlemen from the great Shahbag families took the river air. Sometimes a famous beauty like my grandmother was seated at their sides. Although her face was veiled, her rich garments and most especially her ostrich-feather fan with its jeweled handle revealed to every eye that she was from our haveli.

You see, the courtesans of our haveli were rumored to be even wealthier than the wives of the Nawab. Presents were showered on them by other rulers. Renowned not just for their beauty but for their learning, they were in great demand to educate the heirs to India's mightiest kingdoms.

Are you familiar with Vatsayana's classic, the *Kama Sutra?* No? Read the requirements of a courtesan as Vatsayana describes them. Sixty-four arts she must be mistress of, from architecture to zoology. Painting, flower arrangements, music, languages, philosophy, jewelery, literature, even mathematics. Perhaps we were not as educated as the ladies of the *Kama Sutra*, but we were certainly more accomplished than any other woman in India.

And really the essence of all our arts was a single art only: to teach noblemen good manners. For instance, such things as how to pay a compliment.

What is so difficult about paying a compliment? you might ask. It seems an easy thing to tell a woman she has a pretty face.

You are wrong, gentlemen. Those compliments are accepted by fools from gangs of boys who roam the marketplace. We required a lighter touch, a phrase that could delight and yet contain a barb to remind us that beauty was a passing thing, and love beyond attainment.

To give such compliments is one of the things we taught these princes. But to turn a pretty speech on beauty, a man must be able to perceive beauty. After all, the primary colors are seen by every lout, the ordinary scales heard by every washerwoman who repeats them in her songs while she is beating her clothes on the rocks in the river.

But to teach a prince the subtle grading of color or the microtones of melody, to educate a young man's palate so he becomes an epicure, to introduce him to the alchemy of scents—this was the most demanding part of our education.

You see, we were forbidden to give voice to our instructions. We could only educate by hint, by hide-and-seek, by nuance, always struggling to make of our knowledge something as light and transparent as a soap bubble, keeping it suspended in the air as its colors were admired until our students grasped its fragility.

And when they had understood such refinements, but only then, we sometimes allowed them to touch us.

After all, touch is the most dangerous of the senses, wouldn't you say, sir?

Our establishment was so famous for the rigor of its training that our most brilliant courtesans were sometimes invited by an important king to sing and dance when he was entertaining the Viceroy of India himself. My grandmother was in great demand for such occasions. I can still feel the touch of my grandmother's soft, scented hand stroking my forehead as I lay with my head in her lap, while she described how she had trembled as she waited for the court minister to give her the cue to enter those huge audience chambers with the king on one throne, the viceroy on another grander one, his mighty retinue flanking him down the length of the chamber.

And when she had ended her performance she told me a shadowy figure would sometimes stop her in the corridor and offer her a velvet box in which might rest a lotus blossom fashioned of pearls or a rosebud carved from a diamond solitaire. If she accepted the gift the courtier would beckon her to follow him.

My grandmother wove such magic around those nights. She spoke of being rowed to lake palaces under a star-filled sky. Of gossamer nets hanging over beds strewn with jasmine blossoms. Pearls scattered on the sheets. Arched doorways opening onto balconies below which the water lapped softly against the stone foundations.

Oh, friends, how Shahbag has changed in my lifetime. Where there used to be gardens now we have factories. Our gracious old buildings have been torn down to be replaced by concrete boxes named after politicians. The woods that once ringed the city have been cut down for the shanty-towns of labor colonies. Even the boulevards around our haveli have been overrun so that our view is now only of a bazaar, and we must keep the windows to the west closed because of the smell from the open gutter.

The city is owned by men who believe every human being has a price, and a full purse is power. Trained as scholars, artists, musicians, dancers, we are only women to them, our true function to heave on a mattress and be recompensed by some tawdry necklace flashing its vulgarity on a crushed pillow. When they come to our haveli they throw cigarette cases, watches, dirty bank notes at our feet as we dance, oblivious to the frigidness of our salaams.

How often I used to weep in my mother's arms at the coarseness of our audience, but she would hush my sobs and tell me I would never be soiled by their touch.

What can I say, sir, except to tell you that my mother died and I lost my protection from such men.

But my daughter knew nothing of these matters. Inside the walls of our haveli she still learned the arts that had once kept our reputations burnished throughout the Indian kingdoms.

Teaching my daughter was no task at all. She seemed to contain in her slender form all the aspirations of our haveli. I had only to make a suggestion and she would bring the hint into the full flower of an art. From the bells on her anklets she could teach the impermanence of the world. Through a song she could inspire her listeners to imagine the possibility of perfection.

Knowing from bitter experience that the era of our haveli had passed, I wanted nothing to compromise my daughter's name, and I permitted her to appear only at weddings, or the birth of a son, or before families celebrating the head of their household. So jealously did I guard my daughter's reputation that I succeeded in creating an aura of awe around her until she became famous not just for her beauty but for her modesty.

She was called an angel. You may think it is only the opinion of a mother, but truly, sirs, my daughter was an angel, giving love to all who met her as a child gives love to those who have cosseted and spoiled it because it does not know there is harshness in the world, or ugliness.

When she was only seventeen our member of Parliament requested my daughter to perform at his election meeting in the capital. He told me important people from Delhi would be addressing the meeting, and thinking my daughter might one day need the protection of such powerful patrons, I myself took her to perform that afternoon.

Strangely, I felt a premonition of fear when I saw those thousands of people in the park, shifting in boredom as political speeches echoed from the microphones wired on every tree, but I dismissed it as nerves for my child.

I need not have worried. From the moment a party worker led her to the microphone and she began to sing, my child soothed the crowd into silence.

I don't think even my grandmother could have

controlled that vast audience as my daughter did that afternoon, exciting them, consoling them, giving voice to their longings and their despairs, as if our haveli were expressing itself through her slender form.

She was so innocent in the face of her own power, so overwhelmed by the response to her art when the seething mass of people exploded into applause, that her body shivered in my embrace as I led her from the platform.

Hoping to calm her, I suggested we walk home through the bazaar. As always happens during an election campaign, the bazaar was covered with party posters and campaign flags. Political jingles echoed from loudspeakers lashed onto auto-rickshaws, competing to be heard above the film music blaring out of the tea stalls. While my daughter wandered from shop to shop, I stopped at the side of a street to watch a troupe of folk actors enacting the politician's promises for those who could not read.

And then, sir, my life somersaulted.

The sound of machine-gun fire burst through the noise of the bazaar. I screamed for my child but the street was filled with panic-stricken crowds. People were trampling over each other to get into the shops, shrieking with fear as rounds of bullets tore into the air. Seeing my daughter at the far end of the bazaar, I pushed against the crowd with all my might to reach her, but I was crushed, unable to move. I could only watch as a blanket was thrown over her head.

My daughter's limbs flailed against her captor as he flung her over his shoulder. He turned his face to avoid her clawing nails and, oh, sir, I saw Satan walk this earth at that moment. Then his men were helping him into a jeep, and they were gone, firing their guns in the air.

Rahul Singh took my daughter, sir.

My child has been abducted by the most wanted bandit in the Vindhyas, a man the police fear, a murderer whose name is used even in Shahbag to frighten children into obedience.

Please, sir, do nothing until I hold my daughter safely in my arms again.

CHAPTER ELEVEN

Mr. Chagla looked at me. I averted my eyes, ashamed at my reluctance to assist the old woman.

"The police will not hear of your daughter's escape from us," I assured her. "You are welcome to stay as long as you wish."

"Thank you, sir. You are doing a great kindness to my daughter as well as myself."

Mr. Chagla nodded his round head in approval. "I'll tell the staff to prepare rooms."

The woman covered her face with her hands and her shoulders shook as she began weeping again. "I fear my daughter will have much need of kindness. How could this terrible thing have happened? I did everything to protect my child. With her beauty and her unblemished reputation, she could have married a respectable man. Who will believe in my child's virtue now? Who will accept her as a wife, a girl captured and kept by criminals for two long years?"

I was on the brink of suggesting her daughter might be employed in some capacity in our bungalow but fortunately Mr. Chagla returned, saving me from making such an extravagant offer before I had even met the girl.

He helped the old woman from her chair. "You must recover your strength for tomorrow," he counseled compassionately as he led her up the stairs.

That day we saw no more of our visitor. She remained in her rooms while Mr. Chagla tinkered with the generator and I did an inventory of the leaks that had developed in the roof during the recent downpours. By the time Mr. Chagla had succeeded in restoring our power, the storm had passed and we were able to take advantage of the clear sky to make some minor repairs to the roof. We did not need lights immediately, but I was glad the fans were working and the old lady would get some relief from the oppressive humidity.

To my delight the good weather lasted. The next morning, after many weeks, I was able to go the terrace for my dawn meditations. As I was crossing the gardens, I saw a figure dressed in white slipping through the bungalow gate, and I knew the old woman was already leaving to meet her daughter.

I have always regretted the heavy storms that prevent me from coming to the terrace more often during the monsoons. The Narmada is at its most dramatic during this season. The distant waterfalls, swollen by monsoon rains, crash through the marble rocks like surf breaking at full tide, and below the rest house the river churns and bubbles around sudden rapids, eroding the gray-green stones lying on its riverbed into the oval lingams that are the symbol of Shiva.

For some reason only the rocks in the Narmada riverbed carry the mark denoting the third eye of Shiva and the three lines of his ascetic's ashes, becoming the smooth lingams worshipped in family altars and mighty temples alike with the prayer "In the living stones of the Narmada, God is to be found."

I sat in the darkness repeating the invocation until the first rays of daylight pierced the monsoon mists shrouding the fields across the river. A strong wind was pushing banks of clouds toward our hills. I watched them changing shapes and colors in the sunlight as they raced toward the eastern horizon like herds of animals or the battlements of medieval cities, some yellow, some the color of smoke, some white with the pink blush of conch shells.

By the time I ended my meditations the sky overhead was blue, without a cloud in sight. I decided to take advantage of the fine weather and walk to Tariq Mia's house, curious to hear his reaction to the old woman's story.

A thick undergrowth of ferns had sprung up in the jungle behind the bungalow since my last walk, and water from the previous day's storm still dripped from the luxuriant foliage. I made my way around the puddles in the mud path, avoiding the fallen creepers—blue convolvulus, white jasmine, orange-pink lantana—floating in the water. Monkeys shrieked at my approach from branches overhead, and once I paused to watch a peacock fanning its tail as it performed its mating dance to some peahen, invisible in the distance.

My pleasure at being out of the bungalow was so great I was unaware that I had reached the summit of the hill until I heard a group of village women shouting at me from the Jain caves.

"Sahib, see what we have found!"

"Sahib! Come quickly!"

A woman ran up to me and took my arm, pulling me toward a cave where the other women were crouching over a black bundle.

"We came here looking for dry kindling, and found these."

"What shall we do with them, sahib?"

My hands suddenly felt cold in spite of the heat. Three rifles and two boxes of cartridges wrapped in an oilskin were lying on the mud. "Send your men to call the police from Rudra."

The women watched me wrap the oilskin around the arms, noisily speculating on who had hidden the guns.

"Someone tell Tariq Mia to keep all his villagers inside until he hears from me," I said as they followed me up the hillside. "The rest of you return to your homes and stay there until the police say it is safe to move about again."

When I reached the bungalow, I told the guard to make sure the staff did not wander out of the grounds. He ran outside to see if anyone had left the rest house and I carried the oilskin bundle to my office, certain the weapons were somehow connected with the old woman's daughter.

Opening the steel cupboard in which I keep cash for bungalow emergencies, I stored the guns and boxes of cartridges on a stack of unused files on the bottom shelf. As I was locking the cupboard, the door of my office opened.

A slender young woman stood in the hall. Although she was dressed in a white sari, the homespun cotton gave her almost a royal air as she waited to be invited inside. I could see she had just bathed. The thick black hair hanging loose to her waist was still wet. She kept her gaze demurely away from me but her modesty was magnetic, forcing my eyes to stay on her as her long eyes examined some object on my desk, the lashes brushing against the delicate color of her cheek.

"I came to thank you for your kindness to my mother," she said softly, her low voice pleasing to my ears.

"Your mother?"

"Yes. She met me on the road."

I pulled up a chair, trying to disguise my shock. "Please. Please sit down. Are you all right? Is there anything I can get you?"

She sat down with an economy of movement that did nothing to distract from the suppleness of her slender body or the fluid grace of her actions.

"Would you like some food? Do you need money or—"

"My mother has already taken care of my requirements," she interrupted me gracefully.

I was unprepared for such self-possession and could hardly believe she had undergone her terrible ordeal. "Where is your mother?"

"Resting before our departure. I made her lie down."

"Could you fetch her?"

"Please, sir. She is very tired. Let her rest a little longer."

"I'm afraid I must talk to her urgently."

"Can't I help instead?"

"I don't know. Guns have been found in our jungle. It will take the police an hour to get here, by which time your mother and yourself can be gone. But you must tell me at once if you are being pursued. I am responsible for the safety of my staff."

She looked at me and I thought I saw a flash of defiance cross her expression before she dropped her eyes demurely again. "No one is any danger because of me."

"How do you know your kidnappers are not already on your trail?"

"Perhaps you would believe me if I tell you why I was kidnapped."

She folded her hands on the desk. I could not help noticing the elegance of her slim fingers. Then I saw her nails were bitten down to the quick, and that evidence of nerves moved me in a way her self-control had not. As if reading my response, she suddenly seemed to become a vulnerable young girl.

"It was many weeks before I myself knew the reason for my capture, sir. I can't tell you much about those weeks except that we fled deeper and deeper into the jungles, to some place my captors called the resting place of the Immortal where no police dared follow.

"Of that time I can only remember my exhaustion, and the bitter taste of my fear, and the strange men always nearby so I could hear their coarse laughter and smell the stink of their unwashed bodies even at my most private moments. But through that whole time my worst fear was waiting to be assaulted by the leader of the gang.

"He had a black power that seemed to enclose him like a cloud and he stared at me all the time. Once I saw him wet the edge of his turban to wipe the dust from his face, showing a fair skin under the grime. But I still thought of him as black, as something evil and forbidding. When I heard his men calling him Rahul Singh, terror turned my limbs to stone. Even in Shahbag we knew of Rahul Singh's crimes. After that I tried to hide whenever I saw him watching me. But his eyes were always on me, like a panther stalking a goat."

She pressed her wrists to her temples. For a moment I thought she would swoon, but she smoothed back her hair almost coquettishly and continued.

"Eventually we reached this place where the

Immortal is supposed to sleep. It was desolate. No human dwellings. Only the cry of wild beasts and the shrieking of hyenas. For weeks I had been living in the jungle, fearing snakes each time I lay down. Now I was kept in a cave, like an animal. I begged God then to let me die."

She laughed but there no merriment in the sound. "Unfortunately, I discovered the will to live is stronger than the longing for death. Then one night the thing I most feared happened. Rahul Singh appeared in my cave. He placed a lantern between us and sat down. I hope you never endure such fear as I knew then, sir, as I waited for him to move.

"It seemed hours passed as he stared at me with those eyes red with dust before he finally spoke, saying 'I ask forgiveness for what I have made you suffer.'

"I could not understand the timidity with which this man who inspired fear with his very name was now telling me 'God knows my soul and he knows I would not have exposed you to these indignities. But I live on the run from injustice and you must live like me.'

"I implored him to release me. In my desperation I tried to bribe him. 'My mother is not a wealthy woman. But she will beg or steal to pay a reasonable ransom for me.'

"My words angered him. 'We didn't take you for ransom.'

" 'Then what are you going to do with me?' I whispered, frightened by the rage in his voice.

" 'Don't you know? You, who have been my wife in so many lives before this one? Don't you know?'

" 'No!' I screamed. 'No! Never!' I don't know what I was denying beyond my captor's insanity. I only knew this madman was telling me that I would never be allowed to go home. I screamed and screamed when he said, 'No one will harm you. You are under my protection.' I screamed, thinking I would never be permitted to return to our haveli, never again enjoy the sweet refinements of my old life where each motion, each sound was judged by its appropriateness. I screamed, refusing to believe I would be forced to spend the rest of my life with these coarse criminals. But in that desolate resting place of the Immortal, who was there to hear me?

"I cannot tell you how long I screamed, only that I must have gone mad myself because when I came to my senses I was in a mud hut and village women were taking care of me."

Her thick hair had fallen over her shoulders. She swept it back impatiently, lifting her arms to wind it into a bun at the nape of her neck. The gesture pressed her round breasts against the thin fabric of her sari and I saw a mole on the curve of her throat. Embarrassed that I should be so aroused by her beauty when she was telling me her dreadful story, I lowered my eyes and began rifling through the papers on my desk.

"Surrounded by women again I slowly recovered my wits and began planning my escape, but when I asked the women to help me they only laughed. 'How will you escape Rahul Singh? He knows these hills better than any man alive.'

"I pleaded with them to help me escape this murderer.

" 'Rahul Singh is no murderer!' they shouted at me. 'He has the highest decorations for his valor in two wars with Pakistan. When his soldier's commission ended and he came home, he found his family dead and his lands stolen. No one dared help him. The man who took his land had the protection of the local politicians. Denied justice, Rahul Singh only did what any man of honor would do. He swore vengeance on his family's murderers and killed them all. Of course he has become a hunted man. But he has never harmed anyone who did not deserve it.'

"I told them he had harmed me by stealing me from my family. Again and again I begged them to help me run away. They laughed and showed me all the presents he had left for me. And when he came to take me back to the jungles, they sent me with him as if I were his bride."

I listened, hypnotized by the low voice, but in a way which I could not quite identify I saw the girl's demeanor had changed. Now she was telling her story as if she was acting out a play, her expressions changing as she spoke her captors' words, then her own. She no longer appeared vulnerable as she described the next months when, finding she had no weapons except the weapons of the haveli, she employed every art to make Rahul Singh desire her.

"By then I knew in some part of my mind that the village women were right and he would not touch me without my consent. So I punished him by inflaming his longing for me. Then I laughed at his misery when I showed him how coarse I found him, how lacking in the refinements I admired.

"He endured my hatred and my insults. Each time he went on a raid he returned with a gift for me, although his men told me he had risked his safety in some bazaar to do so. And when he was in the camp he sat outside my cave like a dumb brute enduring my worst cruelties."

Now there was an artifice to her manner that I was beginning to find brittle, even distasteful. Her beauty continued to astonish me, but I saw in her gestures the manipulations of the courtesan, as she told me how Rahul Singh left new clothes and once even a set of anklet bells outside her cave.

"I suppose it was boredom that led me to put on the anklets and practice dancing. He used to stand outside the cave in the dark, watching me as if trying to prove there was a greater art than all my arts, the ability to love someone as he loved me, while I danced as if to amuse myself but really to taunt him.

"One night he could endure my cruelty no longer. Under the trees outside my cave, with no light except that of the stars visible through the thick canopy of leaves, with no sound but the calling of wild animals to contradict him, he shouted at me, 'Don't you know you are mine? You have been mine in many lifetimes but each time I lost you. This time I have unsheathed my dagger before Fate. I will not let you go.'

"He stretched out his arms to me. Suddenly I knew he was speaking the truth, and that night I entered my captor's embrace. Guided by his touch, I learned I had known his body in a hundred lifetimes before he took me again a virgin on the thin cotton quilt which was all that shielded our bodies from the ground."

I stared at her, barely hearing her account

of their secret marriage at the temple of Supaneshwara. I could only think of what her mother would feel when she discovered her innocent child had seduced the Satan who had kidnapped her.

"After the wedding he was afraid the police might capture me in order to capture him, and he wanted me to learn how to use a gun to defend myself when he was away.

"He took me to his private place and taught me how to shoot. We were so happy there, in our solitude. He told me a great warrior slept somewhere close by with honeybees circling his head. He laughed, saying his men thought he was himself immortal because he had been stung by one of those bees. I wanted to be stung by such a honeybee so we could be together forever, and sometimes we set out to search for the warrior but we never found him, distracted by our desire for each other.

"When we returned to camp he left on raids with his men again. I repeated the story of the bees to myself while he was gone to calm my fears for his safety. I knew on each raid he put his life in jeopardy to buy something for me, a veil for my head or a fragrance for me to rub on my wrists.

"He was a strange man, you see. So generous he

did not know he was generous and yet always hesitant to ask anything of others."

I put up my hands to stop her, afraid her story was intended to arouse my sympathy for her captor and distract me from the guns locked in my cupboard. She ignored me.

"Not until I conceived did my husband truly believe I loved him. Then he became reckless. He wanted enough money to go to some distant part of the country where no one had heard of him, where we could grow old like any married couple watching our children play while we sat in the shade of a neem tree.

"On one raid he found himself near Shahbag. Thinking to please me, he went into the bazaar to buy something to remind me of my childhood. He had forgotten that the whole bazaar knew his face. There were still old posters on the walls from the time when he had kidnapped me. Before he could escape the police arrived.

"He was badly wounded in the exchange of gunfire. The others managed to get him back to our camp in the jungle and I sat nursing him through the nights and days. But I knew he was dying. He never once opened his eyes, even to bid me farewell.

"Without him as a leader, the gang could not

continue. We divided what we had and I hid in a village, waiting for my confinement. My grief was too great to sustain the life within me. I lost the child."

She walked to the window and stood there looking at the river for a long time in silence. "Last month I sent a message to my mother. I wanted to return to Shahbag and discover who had wounded Rahul Singh. Then I planned to take vengeance on the men who had killed my husband and my unborn child."

She turned to face me. All the artifice had dropped from her demeanor. Now her eyes had the desperation of a trapped animal. "Perhaps my husband willed you to find my guns. He never wanted me to live his life, on the run from the police. But tell me, sir, how long can I keep our secret?"

"Secret?"

"That I am Rahul Singh's woman. It will not be long before the police find out, and some ambitious policeman accuses me of assisting in my husband's crimes. Can you imagine my fate then? Locked in a cell? A girl known to be a courtesan and a bandit's wife?"

There was a timid tap on the door. I was saved from replying as the old lady entered. She looked much stronger and her eyes glistened with tears of happiness as she thanked me repeatedly for allowing her to stay in the bungalow.

Taking her daughter by the hand, she left my office. I watched them walk across the velvet lushness of the garden's monsoon grass to the gate, two figures dressed in white, the girl's slender arm around the bent shoulders of the older woman.

To my surprise they did not take the path that leads to Rudra. Instead they walked to the cliffs above the river. I could see them in the distance standing under a tree, their heads close together as they talked. Suddenly the girl embraced the old woman and she was gone. I rubbed my eyes in disbelief, but when I looked again there was still only the solitary figure of the old woman supporting herself against the tree, staring down into the river.

An engine sounded in the distance as she sank slowly to the ground, leaning forward to look into the rapid current flowing below the cliff. I realized the police jeep was on its way to the bungalow and I was unsure what to do next. I watched the old lady anxiously, wondering if I should go to her assistance, but to my relief she pulled herself to her feet and made her way slowly up the road to Rudra.

The roar of the jeep's engine was much closer. I unlocked the cupboard and unwrapped the rifles, lining them up in a row on the floor behind my desk. Then I stacked the cartridges next to the guns and sat down behind my desk to wait for the police.

A chain rattled as Mr. Chagla secured his bicycle to the fence outside the rest house. A moment later he entered my office, a mournful expression pulling his chubby features downward. "What a sad occurrence, sir. Simply a tragedy."

"Let's at least hear what the police have to say, Chagla."

"Police! What is the use of police now, sir?" he asked in distress. "I met our visitor on the road. She's going home because her daughter is dead."

"Nonsense, Chagla. The daughter was here, in my office, only half an hour ago."

"It can't be, sir. The old lady said her daughter drowned escaping recapture."

The police jeep braked to a halt at our gates.

"Keep an armed guard at the gates!" the sergeant shouted to his men as he ran across the garden. "Someone round up the staff and ask them if any strangers have been seen in the vicinity."

"What's happening, sir? Why are the police—"

"Quickly, Chagla," I interrupted. "Tell me what the old lady told you before the police join us."

Mr. Chagla paced my office in agitation, moving from window to window to watch the policemen. "She said she saw her daughter drowning, sir. With her own eyes. Can you believe such a tragedy? These police, sir—"

"Did the old lady say anything else?" I urged.

He turned to me in exasperation. "Only that she was happy her daughter had died in the Narmada because she would be purified of all her sins. But why are the police . . ."

Suddenly he saw the rifles on the floor behind my chair. He backed away in bewilderment. "What are you doing with these many weapons, sir?"

Before I could answer the door was flung open. The police inspector strode into my office, calling over his shoulder to the constable following him, "I want an inventory of the arms. Serial numbers, types of cartridge, any signs if they were stolen from an army depot."

He pulled out a notebook and sat down, facing me across my desk. "Now, sahib, start from the beginning. Tell me everything you know."

CHAPTER TWELVE

Sometimes when I think I am becoming too set in my ways I leave the familiar surroundings of my bungalow and spend a day in the temple town of Mahadeo.

I usually arrive in Mahadeo in the afternoon and go straight to the bazaars sprawling behind the stone temples overlooking the river.

When I was a bureaucrat I had no reason to enter a bazaar, since my wife saw to our household requirements and my own infrequent shopping expeditions only took me to air-conditioned stores. Now, as I walk through the streets observing the pleasure on the faces of bargaining customers and the cynicism of the shopkeepers, I am reminded how circumscribed my life has been.

I often lose my way while wandering through the warren of shops built so close together they appear to be almost a single building with balconied bridges crossing the narrow gaps above a man's head. At this hour the shopkeepers are opening their establishments for the evening, and their only customers are farmers' wives choosing glass bangles for their daughters or haggling over the price of a bar of soap with a film star's face on the wrapping.

But at dusk the bazaar takes on the appearance of a fair as Mahadeo's residents arrive to make their purchases. Strings of colored electric lights flicker from the overhead balconies. Children hold clouds of spun sugar to their mouths. Hawkers shout, shaven-headed priests push their way toward the temples on the riverbank, housewives argue, women squeeze wet henna in elaborate patterns onto the hands of giggling schoolgirls, young men slip furtively into shops selling country liquor, white-robed pilgrims hurry to complete their purchases for the evening devotions.

For generations the traders of Mahadeo have lived off the Narmada pilgrimage, measuring piety by gullibility, and it amuses me to watch them sitting cross-legged in shops lit by kerosene lanterns, providing the pilgrims with everything they need and convincing them to buy much they do not need: another box of the most expensive incense, more fragments of saffron-colored cloth, the most expensive of the auspicious gems. Surely, at least a dozen clay lamps to float on the river?

My fascination with the energies exploding inside the bazaar always delays me, and it is usually late by the time I reach the stone steps stretching the length of the thirty temples crowded one against the other on the riverbank.

These shallow steps, maybe twenty of them, lead from the forecourts of the temples down to the water and contain, like the bazaar, a whole world of human activity. Beggars and holy men. Priests instructing the devout on how to make their obeisance to the river. Horoscope readers and palmists. Vendors selling baskets of marigolds to be offered to the idols, or glass paintings of the gods as souvenirs. Women, after their ritual baths, drying their saris on stone steps still warm from the day's heat. Pilgrims pouring oil into clay lamps to float on the river.

Above the steps the temples rise like a city, their forecourts crowded with families entering the sculpted stone arches to make their offerings to the idols, then ringing the temple bells when they reemerge, holding their children up to strike the clappers. While the clanging still resonates in the dark, the families descend to place sweets in front of the beggars and holy men sitting on the steps.

The diversity of the people provides me with a constant source of interest and I often fall into conversation with the pilgrims. Across the river the solitary lights of my bungalow shine like a lighthouse in the blackness of the jungles, inviting me to return and consider what I have learned.

I have found when I am talking to some stranger on these steps I discover things about the river that I never knew before.

For instance, once I was sitting behind a woman who was examining the lurid glass paintings of the gods displayed on a cloth before her while the vendor cajoled her to buy one.

I could not see her face, just the thick hair wound at the back of her slender neck and her elegant fingers holding each painting to the light. I was imagining the beauty of her face, when a child shoved her from behind and the picture dropped from her hand. She reached into her bag to pay for the shattered fragments. The irate seller, still shouting at the child, moved on to another customer.

Seeing the woman stoop to collect the glass fragments before some passerby cut his foot, I went to help her. She turned to thank me and I gasped, astonished that she should be so ugly when I had imagined her so beautiful. A large nose tilted across her almost masculine face to overshadow the thin lips lost in a chin that curved upward like a handle.

"People are always alarmed the first time they see me," she said gently as she took the fragment from my hand.

I could have wept at my own cruelty. "No, no. It was not that at all. I cut my hand with a glass splinter."

"Let me see." She held my hand to the light as she had done the paintings. "There is no cut."

In silence we continued to collect the glass fragments. When we had gathered them all, we put them into a newspaper blowing down the stairs. To my surprise she extracted a piece of glass from the newspaper and sat down on the step to study it. I sat down next to her. She handed the shard to me. It was a crude painting of a woman's torso, the breasts painted in bright pink on an aquamarine background.

She seemed not to notice the vulgarity of the painting. "Can't you see? It's a picture of Shiva's consort, the Goddess Parvati, who performed all those great penances until Shiva returned her love. Don't you think it is only proper that such great love should give birth to music?"

I must have looked perplexed because she said shyly, "Musicians believe that one morning after Shiva had made love to the Goddess all night— and a night in the lives of the gods is thirty thousand years of human time—Shiva rose from his bed and saw the Goddess still asleep. Her breasts were like perfect globes and her slender arm rested across them, her fragile bangles sliding up and down with each breath. Shiva was moved to such tenderness by the sight that he created an instrument to immortalize his wife's immortal beauty—the first instrument of music, the veena.

"Look, the two globes that provide the veena's resonance are the breasts of Parvati. The neck of the veena is her slender arm, the frets of the veena her glass bangles, and the music of the veena the expression of Shiva's love."

I studied the painted torso but could find no trace of beauty in it. She seemed to understand because she said, "Perhaps only genius can see beauty in what appears ugly. My father can. And he is called a genius."

She lapsed into silence. Below us two pilgrims were standing waist high in the dark river, cupping water in their hands then letting it fall in a stream through their fingers as they chanted, "Om. Om. Om."

The woman pointed at them. "My father recites

that every morning before he plays his veena. First he closes his eyes and takes a deep breath. Then, when I think his lungs must burst if he does not exhale, he intones Om, his eyes closed, his body motionless so that only the vibration of his deep voice issues through his lips.

"As I child I thought I could see things in the room shaking with the vibration, although when I looked at them nothing moved. But sometimes I could hear the merest note from a string on his veena, a sound so fragile it disappeared into the air before I could hold it in my memory. Then he would open his eyes and say,

" *'Om is the three worlds.*
Om is the three fires.
Om is the three gods.
Vishnu, Brahma, Shiva.' "

She smiled at me and we continued to listen to the bathers chanting. Suddenly she added, "It sounds like one note. But actually it is three and a half sounds. Can you hear them?"

I listened closely. All I heard was the single note being expelled by the bathers into the night.

"No, listen. It is created by the three separate actions of your body—when you open your lips, when you release your breath, when you close your lips. Try it."

Still embarrassed by my own rudeness when I had first seen her face, I obediently opened my mouth and rounded my lips. I was astonished by the force with which the Om issued from my mouth. As she listened to me she recited,

"The first sound of Om is the manifest world.
The sound of waking consciousness.
The sound of gross experience."

My lips were closed and I could feel the Om vibrating through my nostrils as she recited,

"The second sound of Om is the unmanifest
  world.
The sound of dreaming consciousness.
The sound of subtle experience."

Now I felt my lungs bursting as I struggled to elongate the note beyond her recitation.

"The third sound of Om is the nonmanifest
  world.
The sound of dreamless sleep.
The sound of potential experience."

There was no breath left in my lungs but I still felt my lips vibrating as I took a deep breath while she recited,

"The half-syllable of Om is silence.
The sound of the unmanifest world.
It is the ultimate goal.
The incomparable target."

She laughed when she saw me gasping for breath, and I thought she was trying to make a fool of me to avenge herself on my earlier tactlessness. Annoyed by her experiment, I asked crossly, "Why are you in Mahadeo, anyway?"

"I am on a pilgrimage."

"You are not dressed as a pilgrim."

"Oh, I am not making a religious pilgrimage. This is part of my musical education."

"I thought musicians were supposed to practice, not walk around a river."

"Most musicians do not have the misfortune of having a genius for a teacher."

"And I suppose you are absolutely certain your teacher is a genius?"

"Oh, yes. He is the finest veena player in the world. Our house is always crowded with famous musicians, begging to be my father's students. But he has only ever shared his knowledge twice. With myself . . ."

She fell silent and I watched her wrap the glass fragment in newspaper and place it carefully in her bag.

"And the other?" I asked, unable to restrain myself.

Her large eyes seemed to melt into an inner darkness as she observed sadly, "The other is the reason for my presence here."

Intrigued, I asked her to explain her pilgrimage.

She shook her head. "It would make no sense unless you knew about my father."

"Then tell me about him."

CHAPTER THIRTEEN

THE MUSICIAN'S STORY

It is hard to be the child of genius.

Even when I was very small, not yet three years old, I was aware that my father dwelt in some other sphere as if he had struck a bargain with God that took him outside human boundaries.

No one stopped me when I lay on the floor outside his music room because I never made a sound as his fingers moved across the frets of his veena forming shapes in the air, a whole architecture of sound that I could walk through and around, so substantial when I listened that I believed it would last for a thousand years.

I always wondered as a child, where did such beauty go? Which audience of spirits sat waiting for the sounds to rearrange themselves into arches, vaults, balconies, spires, domes that they could inhabit? But I could not ask my father. He was surrounded by musicians, their silent applause flowing around him as impassable as deep water as they listened to his genius taking him toward some unknown dimension on the ladder of music that he was constructing so painstakingly with his veena.

Whenever I tried to approach my father, that sea of adulation closed like water over my head before I was able to reach the smiling figure glancing at me with indifferent interest as if I were a pi-dog puppy who had wandered into his music room. I don't think it could be said of my father that he was sensitive to the presence of other human beings unless they intruded on his music, so he never noticed me. But he noticed my despair.

You see, despair is an emotion, and the emotions were like shoals of brilliant fish swimming through his melodies. Or colored gases floating through the ether in which his music dwelt.

To the entire household's astonishment, when I was six years old my father, who had never accepted a student from all the great musicians who had begged to sit at his feet, stretched out his hand, making a bridge for me to cross the gulf of praise that separated us, and offered to teach me music.

My first music lesson extended for several months. In all that time I was not permitted to touch an instrument. I was not even permitted to sing the seven notes of the scale: the *sa, re, ga, ma, pa, dha, ni* that are the *do, re, mi, fa, so, la, ti* of western music.

Instead my father made me sit next to him in the evenings as the birds were alighting on the trees.

"Listen," he said in a voice so hushed it was as if he was praying. "Listen to the birds singing. Do you hear the half notes and microtones pouring from their throats? If I practiced for ten lifetimes I could not reproduce that careless waterfall of sound and sshh . . . listen closely."

I tried to imitate him, bending forward in my chair. "Hear? How that song ended on a single note when the bird settled into the tree? The greatest ragas must end like that, leaving just one note's vibrations on the air."

I nodded in enthusiasm, hoping to please him, but he did not see me. "Do you know why birds sing at dawn and at sunset? Because of the changing light. Their songs are a spontaneous response to the beauty of the world. That is truly music."

Then he told me that he would die happy if he were able to create such music five or ten times in a whole lifetime.

"Men are fools," my father said as we walked in the jungles behind our house. "They think only humans respond to beauty. But a feeding deer will drop its food to listen to music, and a king cobra sway its hood in pleasure. Listen. Do you hear that peacock's cry? It is the first note of the scale. *Sa.*"

Standing under the trees we waited to hear the peacocks cry again, and when they did my father's voice echoed them and the peacocks fell silent, listening.

It seemed to me that we were wandering only for pleasure in the fields around our house or in the jungles. I did not realize my father was teaching me the seven notes of the scale as described in the classic texts.

But at sunset we waited until the cowherds were driving their cattle back to their villages and my father said, "Can you hear that calf calling its mother? It is the note—*re.*"

We watched my mother throwing vegetable peelings to the goats in our back field. "Hear the goats? If you sing *ga* three times, very quickly, it is the bleating of a goat."

We waded into the paddy fields behind the herons. "*Ma,* the cry of the heron."

At night, "*Pa,* the song of the nightingale."

In the bazaar streets as we followed the horse carriages, *"Dha*—the neighing of a horse."

And when the circus came to town, my father was excited at the opportunity of teaching me the last note of the scale. "Can you hear that *ni*—when the elephant trumpets?"

Then my father sang the notes of the scale so I could hear him imitating the animals we had seen —the strutting of the peacock, the panic of a lost calf, the destructive antics of a goat, the sweeping flight of the heron, the nightingale nesting in a tree, the rearing of a horse, the power of an angry elephant—until the nature of the notes became second nature to me. He also sang the ragas in which each note predominated so that my uneducated ear became familiar with all the major ragas before I ever held in an instrument in my hands.

"There was no art until Shiva danced the Creation," he said, explaining how melody was born. "Music lay asleep inside a motionless rhythm— deep as water, black as darkness, weightless as air. Then Shiva shook his drum. Everything started to tremble with the longing to exist. The universe erupted into being as Shiva danced. The six mighty ragas, the pillars of all music, were born from the expressions on Shiva's face, and through their vibrations the universe was brought into existence.

"The melodies of these six ragas sustain the harmonies of living things. When they fuse together they become the beat of Shiva's drum that brings the universe to destruction. But they are all male. And music can never be still, it can never be without desire. Life must create more life or become death. So each of the six ragas was given six wives, six raginis to teach them love. Their children are the putras, and in this way music lives and multiplies."

Then my father said I must see the emotions through which ragas and raginis communicated with each other. "Each raga is related to a particular season, a time of day, an emotion. But emotion is the key that unlocks a raga's soul."

So, every day for a month, we went together to the dance academy to study Shiva's dance of Creation. I watched girls my age struggle to convey emotions that they had never known but that were the basic moods of dance: Laughter, Wonder, Heroism, Anger, Grief, Pity, Love, Fear, Tranquility.

Sometimes I laughed at their inability to put sufficient gravity into their moods, and my father was displeased.

"Don't treat the arts so lightly. They are Shiva's gifts to mankind. If you choose to be a musician, you enter into a pact with Shiva himself. Remember, every note you play sends new music into the universe. You can never reclaim it."

I thought my father was speaking to himself because I did not understand his meaning. But at last I was able to ask the question that had always been in my mind. "And where does all that music go?"

"It returns to the sound that is so all-encompassing it is silent, the sound we call the secret of the Gandharva Veda."

"Have you ever heard it?"

"No, but every day I listen for it when I play. You must listen for it too. The Vedas say that by playing the veena with the correct rhythm, keeping its notes and its character intact, a man can hear that sound and attain salvation."

Then my father took me to the small street of painters that stretched at one side of the town temple to watch the artists grinding their colors with stones. He was always searching for ways to make me understand the link between my music and the world, and while I peered over the artists' shoulders he taught me which ragas they would be painting from the small pots of colors they were placing before their paper—*sa* was black, *re* was tawny, *ga* was gold, *ma* white, *pa* yellow, *dha* indigo, *ni* green.

That portrait of a man with black skin carrying

in his hand a sharp-edged sword to slash through the clouds like lightning was Megh, the raga of rain. That man with flames around his head, riding a savage elephant to show fire's power, was Deepak, the raga of heat. That girl fanning herself with a peacock's feather as she drank from a goblet was Vaulika; that maiden lying in front of a hut on the grass with a garland in her hands was Desi; that girl talking to her deer as she took them home at evening was Todi.

By the time six months were over I could recite the moods that each raga created and its seasons, and identify them in the pictures I saw being painted in the street.

Still, an entire year passed before my father finally allowed me to take the veena across my knees.

I was so small the instrument stretched beyond both sides of my body and my crossed legs didn't even touch the arm. My father instructed me to place both hands on the strings without making a sound.

"Always treat your instrument with humility. After all, what is a raga? Five notes, seven. If you add some halftones, maybe twelve. It is only a skeleton of melody. And the veena is only two gourds attached by a piece of wood and a handful of wires. But when they are united, and you create a composition from their union, it must speak the language of the soul. You see, a raga has its own soul. Without its soul, its rasa, a raga is only a dead thing."

He warned me I must respect each note of music so that I could give it life. "Once there was a great musician who boasted all the time that he could play better than anyone else. One day the notes of the scale turned into seven nymphs and walked past as he was playing. Suddenly one nymph fell to the ground, dead. The musician was playing his instrument so violently that he strangled the note in his strings. He murdered the nymph with his pride."

I started crying, fearing my father would somehow blame me for the nymph's death. He only smiled at my distress and continued his story. "As the musician was staring in horror at the dead woman in front of him, a holy man passed by and asked if he could borrow the instrument. He played on it so sweetly he brought the note-nymph back to life. That is how you must try to play."

And then at last my father allowed me to pluck the primary scale from the strings of my veena. For half an hour he listened to me play as closely as if he were listening to a great musician before stopping me. "The first sound of creation was Om.

Each vibration of Om created new sounds that led to the primary scale. Think of these seven notes as the Om of music. If you cannot play them correctly you will never be able to master a raga."

I was only a child but my father wanted me to understand that music was the mathematics by which the universe could be comprehended. Morning after morning, month after month he made me play the *sa, re, ga, ma, pa, dha, ni* over and over again, one hand moving up and down the frets, the other plucking at the veena's strings, until my fingers bled. He ignored my tears and forced me to continue practicing until the cushions of my fingertips developed calluses. But still he was not satisfied with the clarity of my notes.

If my mother had been more sympathetic I would have asked her then to end my music lessons. Unfortunately, my mother seldom spoke to me. My ugliness upset her. When other children stared at me, sniggering at my ugliness, my mother's eyes filled with tears but she never comforted me or told me they were wrong.

Shamed by mother's tears, I hid in the bathroom, examining myself in the mirror to see if my face was losing any of its coarseness. Each time I looked I saw only two features in the mushy flesh, this nose growing bigger as if trying to join this chin that drives forward like a fighter's, tempting an opponent's attack.

My father was oblivious to my ugliness. After listening to me practice on my veena he would play himself, making me learn the scales that formed the ragas. For two years these skeletons of melody were all I learned. My father would play some notes and ask me what he was playing. When I identified the raga he would recite a sacred saying peculiar it.

"A goddess presides over each of the ragas. If you truly meditate on a raga's sacred teaching, its goddess will give you mastery over its melodies."

I stared at him resentfully as he spoke, hating his nose and chin because they were exaggerated so cruelly on my own face. He was not a handsome man, but at least his features were in proportion to his face, and his naturally austere expression lent them distinction. I wanted him to give me a sacred saying, a goddess who would grant me beauty.

Perhaps I did my father an injustice. Through music he tried to free me of my own image so I could love beauty wherever it was to be found, even if it was not present in my mirror.

Then one day when I was eleven years old, my father gave me a picture of a man with matted hair and snakes clasping his forehead above his three eyes.

"This is the raga you will learn. The Bhairav. Bhairav is another name for Shiva, meaning the Fire of Time."

My hands trembled as I held the picture of the god, his body smeared with ashes, a drum and a trident in his hands. I had been under my father's instruction for five years by now. At last my father felt I was capable of commencing the performance of a raga.

At that very moment my mother began to sit outside the music room as a jailer waits for a prisoner. I was not gifted enough for my mother to feel secure about my future. She had lived so long with genius that she could recognize it like a bazaar fruit seller recognizes a fine mango from a merely good one even though he has not grown it, and she believed that a woman without genius could be protected only by a husband in a harsh world designed for men.

When I finished my music lesson she forced me to endure teas with her friends and their sons. I could see the boys recoiling from my ugliness, but my mother's resolve to see me safely married only hardened as, week after week, the teas progressed and no offers were made for my hand.

How can I describe my anguish in the years that

followed, as I struggled to please my father inside the music room, and then outside the music room consoled my mother for my ugliness.

On one side was my father's invitation to wander freely in the fields of music, where even a child like myself could fall on cushions of melody, run across bridges of notes, swing on the stretch of the veena's strings, make garlands of different-colored notes to place before the goddesses of the ragas. But outside the room I saw my mother's face creased with worry, my ugliness reflected in her eyes.

By now my body was beginning to show its maturity, changes that I could not overlook if only because the weight of the veena was too much against my budding breasts. With these changes in my physique had come a change in my emotional state. My senses felt everything too strongly. I no longer swam with the freedom of a dolphin through the caverns of my father's music. I was too preoccupied with my own ugliness and my mother's despair, my uncertain future looming before me as mysterious as the changes of my body.

Suddenly my father decided he no longer wanted to teach me. "You make too much music. A raga is not composed of notes. It is composed of the silence between the notes."

Once I would have wept openly at my father's words. Now I lowered my eyes so that he would not see my great shame. My pain attracted my father's attention. Or perhaps it was my silence that made him relent.

"I will continue to teach you. But on one condition. They say the greatest gift a man can give is the gift of a daughter in marriage. If you insist on studying under me, you must be prepared to be a bride."

It seemed to me that I could not escape the specter of marriage. Knowing no man would want me as a wife, I begged him to continue my musical education.

"Think carefully before you say yes," my father warned. "Remember, if I teach you the raginis I will be giving you as wife to my gods, the gods of music. Such a contract cannot be broken. It will be a marriage sealed by Shiva himself."

I humbly assured him I understood, and my father continued my education.

Now my father's lessons lifted me into another universe.

He changed my instrument from the veena to the more pliant sitar, hearing in that softer instrument my yearning for beauty as he taught me the grace notes that distinguish the great musician from a student.

"Imagine a raga as a riverbed. The grace notes are the water of the river. It is written in the *Raga-vivodha* that a raga without grace notes is like a night without moonlight, a river without water, a creeper without flowers, a woman without a garment."

He taught me the subtleties of tenderness, how to be supple before gravity, how to gentle anger, how to seduce and sigh and caress through my music.

"You must think of yourself as water washing over stone, shaping it with the relentless touch of your love. Think of yourself as silk that disguises its strength in softness. The force of your desire, the heat of your longing must melt the rigidity of the raga."

My sensibilities became so refined under my father's tutelage that when he recited to me the contemplations of differing raginis, I could immediately visualize them.

"Here is the contemplation for Lilavati. She is of sixteen summers, she wears ropes of pearls, she carries a lotus, and she speaks of love to her confidantes while she waits for her beloved.

"The lilting Madhu-madhavi has a golden complexion and is of incomparable beauty. She is seated laughing with her lover on a swing at springtime.

"The yearning Shyam-Gujari stands in a moon-lit garden telling a peacock of her longing for her lover.

"Here is the contemplation of Bhairavi. The appointed hour of her tryst has passed and her lover has not appeared. She tears off her jewels and the flowers in her hair. She smears her body with ashes, grieving for the loss of her beloved.

"Here is the contemplation of Barari. Her robes are white, her hair is like monsoon clouds, her waist is narrow, her navel deep as a lake, her fragrance as sweet as a lotus. Butterflies follow her as she runs to her beloved."

Just think what my study did to me, an adolescent girl who knew the stain of her ugliness would prevent any man from desiring her, and yet learning only how to express longing.

But I cannot say that mine was an unhappy life. I had already experienced one miracle when my father undertook my musical education. Now the second miracle happened.

It was evening, the time when my father played to the gods. None of us could disturb him but sometimes I passed near the room to listen.

This evening I stopped to look through the doorway of his music room, never having heard my father play this way before. To my surprise I saw a young man sitting below my father's platform playing the veena. He was dressed as a supplicant, bare-footed, his torso naked except for the instrument resting against his bare shoulder. I stared in wonder at his slanting eyes, at his black hair falling softly to the strong line of his neck, at the muscled arm as his fingers moved across the frets of his instrument. He was so beautiful I shut my eyes against his power, thinking I had imagined him in my long training in desire. When I opened my eyes I still saw him, and it was as if ten thousand honeybees had stung my heart at once.

I don't know how long I stood there, but finally the young man laid his instrument at my father's feet.

"Will you accept me as a student?" he asked humbly.

My father did not bother to disguise his impatience. "Everyone knows I have never taken a pupil, except for my daughter."

"Then let me live here, so I can listen to you play. I will serve your food or heat the water for your bath. I will perform the most menial tasks if only you permit me to be near you."

"Are you so willing to do anything to be taught by me?"

"The more rigorous your terms, the happier I will be to accept them."

"Music is not allied to pain. You will not be a

better musician if you suffer more than other men."

"Just tell me what you require of me and I will do it."

"If I teach you, will you take my daughter as your wife?"

"Is that all? Willingly."

My father lifted his hand to beckon me into the room, and the stranger turned. I saw the shock on the stranger's face, as if he could not believe my father could sire such ugliness.

At that moment I wished my father dead. He did not see the stranger's disbelief, and if he had my father would not have cared. Genius stands at a strange angle to the world of humans, careless of its own cruelty.

And what refinement of cruelty it was. Day after day my ugliness faced the stranger's beauty as my father taught us.

Locked in my hatred of my father, I could not bring to my instrument that longing which I had perfected when there was no one there.

My awkward playing made the stranger's music more unforgiving, so that the notes of his raga had an iron hardness that forbid approach.

My father was enraged at his insensitivity. "The ragas are the architecture of emotion. Have you never known weakness or fear? Are you so stupid?"

I wept within myself for the stranger's pain at my father's harsh criticisms. But my father was relentless. "Any pedant can learn a raga's melody. It is only a matter of practice. Music goes beyond technique. The Boddhistava broke every string of the veena, one by one, and still the raga continued, vibrating in the waters of human emotion."

The stranger did not yet know his own genius, only his talent and his ambition, and my father eroded that ambition with ruthless skill.

"Your tastes are too cheap to play the great ragas. You are content to create mere pleasure. Didn't your last teacher teach you the Upanishads:

" *'The better is one thing, the pleasant another.*
  Both aims may bind a man.
  But the wise man chooses the better over the
    pleasant'?"

Then my father turned to me, his fury at my incompetence as great as his anger at the stranger's lack of imagination.

"What are the two emotions that govern the two sexes in all music?"

"The heroic for the man. The erotic for the woman," I whispered, fearful of drawing the stranger's eyes to my face.

My father raised his hands in the air in front of him as if beseeching the gods. "What am I to do with these lumps of clay? From the outside they look like a man and a woman. Why are they not alive?"

We were betrothed, my father's two students. And yet we never spoke to each other except in stilted greetings and farewells.

My father spoke for both of us, haranguing us to become more than we were, not allowing us to hide our shame from him or from each other.

Once he took the veena from the stranger's shoulder when he was again displeased by the boy's playing. "Do you know what this instrument is? Look at the curve of its neck. Its breasts, its slender arm. This is the expression of Shiva's love. Can't you imagine a woman? Or love?"

Day after day, lesson after lesson, he shamed us, forcing us to understand the meaning of being a man and a woman.

But what we learned most from him in those years was the blessedness of silence, when we were neither struggling to please him with our instruments nor listening to his voice harshly reminding us of our errors.

Over the months my father's fury made us conspirators. Fearing his anger at one student would be deflected on the other, we began helping each other, trying to read the other's mistake before it was made, increasingly conscious of each other's moods.

Now I remembered my father's teachings as I tried to be the water to the river of the stranger's raga, the moonlight to his night. And when I thought how my father had said that a raga without the waterfall of grace notes was like a woman without a garment, I tried to teach the stranger what a woman felt, pleading for his attention by extending the notes pulled from the strings of my sitar so he could hear the ache in me.

Suddenly it was as if I had gained a voice to tell the stranger of my pain at my own ugliness, of my remorse that he should have been locked into this unjust bargain of marriage by my father.

I do not know where I learned such duplicity or if I always harbored it in my soul, but I began seducing the stranger with my weakness and he grew heroic in his music to defend me from my father's contempt.

As silk disguises its strength in softness, as water erodes the unforgiving nature of stone, as flesh embraces steel, I embraced the music of the stranger's veena and through the strings of my sitar I told him that I dared to love his beauty. Slowly, oh how slowly, the stranger's music began responding to the request in mine until we were no longer conscious of my father's presence in the room, only hearing the pleading of my ragini to be the wife of his lordly raga, the silences between our notes growing electric with desire.

Sometimes I saw the stranger's eyes linger on some part of my body left exposed by my garments and I did not hasten to cover myself, pretending I had not noticed his attention wandering from my music. I even began to hope I was not as offensive as I had always believed myself to be. We were young, you see, we were a man and a woman, and we could not pass our days in the constant dialogue of desire without being overwhelmed by it.

But my mother was growing impatient for our marriage to be performed. The stranger was by now twenty-one years old, I was eighteen. Every day she demanded that my father set a date for the wedding, yet my father hesitated. I had never seen him indecisive in his life. I could not understand why he bargained each day with my mother to delay the marriage he had himself demanded from his student.

Finally he told my mother, "Let them play together on the night of Shiva. Then we will choose a date."

That year, as always happened on the night of Shiva, our house was filled with musicians. All night the musicians played, one after another or sometimes together, waiting for the moment when my father would lift his veena and praise his gods with his genius.

But this year my father told the assembled musicians that tonight his students would play for them. Then he invited us to join him on the platform.

It was the hour to play the Bhairav, the raga of Shiva, when darkness turns into dawn. The stranger played the opening movement of the raga. My father nodded in approval listening to the stranger slowly unfold the raga's divinity, carving a great stone temple of music in the air. I understood my father's harangues against what is only pleasant in music as the magnificence of the raga was displayed to us, becoming ever more grave, more monumental, more relentless, as if embodying its name, the Fire of Time.

And now I disturbed its mighty solitude with the sacrifice of Parvati wooing Shiva from his asceticism, pleading that he love her. And so we played together, as the darkness turned into filigreed shadow, and still we played until there was light in the room, and still we played as the sun showed its power, until exhausted by the consummation of our music we ended together on a single note, as if consigning our music to the silence that followed it.

When even my father could no longer hear that last note vibrating in the air, he rose to his feet. "Tonight I gave my daughter in marriage to music. I have fulfilled my duties as a father. Now I free this young man from our bargain. But if he still wishes marry my child, the wedding can take place whenever my wife wishes."

The stranger smiled at me as my mother placed a garland of flowers around his neck. I dared not look at him in case my joy overflowed, flooding my eyes.

And so the stranger left our house to return to his family while my mother made preparations for our marriage.

For the first time I preferred my mother's company to my father's. We collected my trousseau and decorated the rooms in which my bridegroom and I would live as man and wife.

The priest was organized, an auspicious night was chosen for our nuptials. We sent shawls and saris for my bridegroom's parents.

Every day my mother speculated on the progress of events. The bridegroom's family should be arriving soon, the red invitations with the gold lettering must have reached their destinations.

Then at last a messenger arrived from my bridegroom's family.

My mother and myself hid outside my father's music room, whispering excitedly to each other as the messenger unwrapped gifts below my father's platform.

I looked at the shawls piling up at my father's feet and recognized them as the gifts we had sent to my bridegroom's family, but I still did not understand what was happening until I heard the messenger say, "Your student thanks you for granting his freedom. He is betrothed in marriage to my daughter."

From that moment I have not touched my instrument nor entered my father's music room. The very sound of music is hateful to my ears.

So my father has brought me here.

He says that I must meditate on the waters of the Narmada, the symbol of Shiva's penance, until I have cured myself of my attachment to what has passed and can become again the ragini to every raga.

He says I must understand that I am the bride

of music, not of a musician. But it is an impossible penance that he demands of me, to express desire in my music when I am dead inside.

Do you think it can be done?

Do you think this river has such power?

CHAPTER FOURTEEN

"Well, do you think so?" Tariq Mia asked, gazing placidly at the brook below the bridge racing downstream to join the Narmada.

I glanced at him in disbelief. "Of course not. The beauty of the Narmada makes it a perfect retreat for anyone like myself wishing to withdraw from the world. But how can it exorcise a lover's grief?"

I was sitting on Tariq Mia's veranda, enjoying these last days of fine weather before summer overwhelmed us, telling him of my encounter at Mahadeo.

Wisps of white smoke from the village houses behind us floated toward the river and squirrels streaked up and down the marble platform leading to Amir Rumi's tomb. Above the mosque the purple blossoms of a jacaranda tree waved gently against the brilliant blue of a late April sky.

It was such a glorious morning I could not understand why I was suddenly overcome by a sensation of—how shall I describe it—being adrift in the strangeness of other people's lives, but I seemed unable to stop my account from turning into a complaint.

I stared at the chessboard lying idle between Tariq Mia and myself.

"I suppose all this emotion alarms me." I ended lamely, "Broken engagements, unrequited love, that poor musician. It all strikes me as somehow undignified."

"You still know so little of the world," the old mullah observed, his eyes on the brook. "But you have chosen a hard path to knowledge, little brother. Hearsay, not experience. I hope your education proves less painful than your musician's."

"Why shouldn't it? My father, a most reasonable man, is already dead. And at least I don't dread my mirror."

"Destiny is playing tricks on you. Don't you realize you were brought here to gain the world, not forsake it?"

The old priest's complacency annoyed me. "I

know the world well enough. Sitting in your isolated mosque you can have little idea of the power
and influence I once wielded. Or the respect I enjoyed."

Tariq Mia laughed at my indignation. "I still
say you should envy your musician, not pity her.
Think of your misfortune. To hear of love without
ever having melted in its embrace. To acknowl-
edge beauty with your eyes and never carry its
image in your soul. Sing with me if you dare,

'O Beloved, can you not see
Only Love disfigures me.' "

I hate it when Tariq Mia is in this mood, and I
examined the chess piece in my hand wondering
why I walked so far each morning to listen to his
quavering old man's voice singing love songs so
inappropriate to his age. My irritation only fueled
Tariq Mia's mischievousness.

"For years you have been admiring the
Narmada as if it is a woman. But what has all your
adoration taught you? Not even the capacity to
sing. Prove me wrong, sing with me,

'Forests heavy with wild jasmine
Embrace you with their fragrance.' "

I pushed the chessboard aside and stood up. "I am not a child. Play these games with your students."

Tariq Mia lifted a lined hand to restrain me. "Sit down, little brother. Don't abandon me to my students yet. The young believe they understand the world. My games are for older men."

Ashamed of my display of ill humor, I was about to resume my seat when he exasperated me by singing again,

"O river, born of penance
Named by laughter,
Forests heavy with wild jasmine . . ."

Then I grasped the purpose of Tariq Mia's teasing.

"That's a song about the Narmada!" I interrupted. "You've never sung it before. Where did you learn it?"

Tariq Mia giggled with pleasure at surprising me. "From the minstrels who sing for the ascetics meditating on the banks of the river."

"Have you heard them often?" I asked enviously as I sat down. "Can you arrange for me to hear them sing?"

"Alas, it has been years since I last saw the Naga Baba. He may be dead by now."

"Is this Naga Baba a minstrel?"

"No, no. He belongs to the martial ascetics, the ones they call the Naga sadhus, the Protectors. But I first heard the invocation to the Narmada from his lips."

I wondered if Tariq Mia was about to make me the target of another joke, comprehensible only to himself. "How did you meet a martial ascetic?"

"By chance. Shortly after I became a priest." Tariq Mia leaned back on his bolster cushion and stroked his thin beard, memory softening the expression in his sharp eyes.

"Imagine me as a young man, little brother. In those days I used to take my books down to the riverbank and look for a teak tree or a bamboo cluster to shade my head. Then, making certain no one could hear me, I practiced singing the Sufi poems. For some reason, whenever I was near the river, my texts became clearer to me, and I wandered all over the riverbank in search of solitude to pursue my studies.

"One day, as I was roaming the hillside, I heard a deep voice chanting in the distance. I followed the sound until I reached the waterfalls but I found no one there. I looked all around me, even up in the trees, and still I couldn't see anyone although I could hear the words clearly from the direction of the waterfalls,

" '*Drop by transparent drop,*
   Each weighted with our separate sins,
   You flow into the ocean's surging tides
   O holy Narmada.'

"I stared at the rock ledge in front of me, unable to understand how the voice could be coming out of the waterfall itself when another voice, so high-pitched it had to be a woman or a child, came through the water,

" '*Messenger of Passing Time,*
   Sanctuary and Salvation,
   You dissolve the fear of time.
   O holy Narmada.'

"Unable to control my curiosity, I took off my shoes and slipped down the ledge in my bare feet until I was standing directly in front of the fall. Now I was close enough to see these voices did not belong to some supernatural being. Through the splashing water I could make out two figures sitting inside a cave behind the falls, as dry as anything while I was being drenched in spray.

"A child of seven or eight years of age dressed in a torn cotton dress was facing a naked man with long matted hair while he recited,

" 'Turtles and river dolphins find refuge in your
*   waters*
Alighting herons play upon your tranquil
*   surface.*
Fish and crocodiles are gathered in your
*   embrace.*
O holy Narmada.'

"As the child repeated the lines, the ascetic turned his face toward the waterfall. That is when he saw me.

" 'How dare you disturb us?' he shouted, throwing his matted locks back from his face. 'What do you want? Who are you?'

"I splashed through the water to present myself, even though I knew these Naga ascetics were famous for their bad tempers, and the child ran to hide in the recesses of the cave. 'Nobody. Just the mullah of a village mosque.'

" 'You have terrified her! Now I will not be able to teach her for the rest of the day!'

"I stood there dripping water onto the stone floor of the cave, uncertain what to say next, when he inquired in an educated voice, 'Did you see any cattle on your way here?'

"I was so astonished by his question that I could only nod in silence.

" 'Where? Where?'

" 'On the hill,' I stuttered, alarmed by the menace in his voice. 'I saw cows on the hill above.'

" 'Come out,' the ascetic called to the child. 'Don't be frightened. Go and collect some cow dung.'

"The child appeared timidly from the shadows, carrying a cane basket and a pile of leaves. The ascetic plucked the leaves one by one from her small hands and lined the inside of the basket.

"I was fascinated by the gray ash falling in a thin powder off his stomach each time he moved. I had never been this close to an ascetic of Shiva before. His body was emaciated, except for the belly falling over his crossed legs in such a manner it was impossible for me to see whether he was completely naked or wearing a loincloth. I think I would have been frightened by the smoke-stained human skull cut open at the cranium lying by his side if he had not placed a pair of rimless glasses on its nose. The sight was so incongruous I nearly burst into laughter.

"Holding the basket on her head with both hands, the child passed through a gap in the waterfall at the edge of the cave. When she was gone the ascetic demanded, 'What do you want of me, mullah?'

" 'Nothing, please forgive my intrusion. I must be getting back to my village.'

" 'You will remain until the child returns.'

"I did not want to upset him further so I said, 'Oh, of course. Certainly. Whatever is convenient.' He closed his eyes and I just sat there looking at him breathe. When he opened his eyes again I asked nervously, 'What were you teaching the child?'

" 'Shankarcharya's poem to the Narmada.'

"To my surprise the ascetic began reciting the invocation to me in Sanskrit. Unable to understand the words, I could only listen to the cadences of his recitation and I imagined I heard the river flowing in the rhythms of the poem.

"Then he courteously explained the invocation to me. The elegance of his translation made me wonder what he had been before he became an ascetic—an academic perhaps, or even a scientist with his grasp of the botanical terms he was using to explain the plants mentioned in the ancient poem."

Tariq Mia paused, breathless from his long account. Only the cry of the rain fever bird broke the morning silence until a young scholar in a long white tunic and pajamas entered the veranda to inquire shyly if there was anything we needed.

The old mullah asked for some hot tea before turning back to me. "So, little brother. That was how I first heard the song of the Narmada."

"Did you see the child again?"

"Oh, yes. I talked with the Naga Baba for a long time until the child returned. I shall never forget the fear in her eyes when she saw me still sitting behind the waterfall."

"Why was she so frightened of you?"

"Are you sure you want to know?" Tariq Mia's white eyebrows lifted above his sharp eyes and hooked nose, so that he looked for an instant like an aging bird of prey.

I laughed, embarrassed by my earlier complaints. In silence we watched the scholar fill our cups with hot tea. As the scholar backed out of the veranda, the old mullah began his story.

CHAPTER FIFTEEN

THE MINSTREL'S STORY

The nine days that precede the night of Shiva were approaching, and the Naga Baba prepared to leave the jungle in search of a cremation ground.

He dismantled the leaf structure in which he had lived for a year, placing the thatched leaves and four poles between a tree's forking roots for some passing mendicant to construct a shelter. Then the Naga Baba took his iron trident wrapped in saffron cloth, his remaining stick of sandalwood, his skull bowl, and began to walk toward the nearest town.

Today the Naga Baba knew he would only need to walk thirty miles or so before he found a cremation ground. But in the early years of his austerities he had sometimes walked two hundred miles before encountering human beings.

Then he had always been exhausted, not knowing which roots and berries to look for in the jungle, or which plants could suppress thirst and hunger, or which yogic exercises slowed down the metabolism so a man could endure the extremes of heat and cold.

Now the Naga Baba was able to center his mind on his meditations no matter how severe his physical discomfort, so he did not notice the distance he was covering or the heat of the tarred road under his bare feet.

As he walked the Naga Baba thought about the harsh disciplines he had undergone to reach his present state.

He remembered the time his teacher had led him into the highest passes of the Himalayas and left him at a small stone temple cut into the mountain rock.

"If you are still alive after the winter," his teacher had said, "I will come for you."

The Naga Baba still could not bear to think of that winter—the hallucinations brought on by his solitary contemplations of death; the blizzards and the dwindling supplies of food that he had eaten raw because there was no wood to light a fire. The rodents dying in front of him as he meditated, their bodies frozen stiff by cold.

But at last the snows had melted. He had been overjoyed to see his teacher standing at the door of his temple, believing the worst of his ordeals was over.

He had not known his teacher would make him cross India on a journey so long the Naga Baba would forget what snow looked like by the time they reached the sand dunes and blowing tumbleweeds of the desert.

"You cannot be a Naga without overcoming human limitations," his teacher had said, leaving him again. "Learn to survive without water. If I find you here when I return, I will take you to our academy."

Now the prospect of sitting in the cremation ground without food or water for nine days no longer frightened the Naga Baba as it once had done. But he could see fear on the faces of the people crossing the road to avoid him. He knew his skin, gray under its daily application of ash, his matted hair falling to his waist in untidy knots, the human skull from which he ate and drank, were all terrifying reminders of death to ordinary people. He also knew they believed he possessed superhuman powers, the ability to levitate and to place irrevocable curses on any who displeased him.

The thought of their fear made the Naga Baba smile as he walked toward the funeral pyre still smoking on the banks of a small stream.

"Jai Shankar! Praise to Shiva!" a man shouted. It was the Dom who tended the funeral pyres, forced to live at the cremation ground because he was considered unclean.

The Naga Baba untied a corner of the saffron cloth covering his trident and took out a pinch of ash to smear in blessing on the Dom's forehead. To ordinary people the very shadow of the Dom was an evil omen, but to the Naga Baba the Dom was a kindred spirit, facing death daily as he did in his own meditations.

Then the Naga Baba cleared his mind of all distraction and prepared to meditate on the God of Death.

He went down to the stream to bathe. With the water still dripping from his body, he sat beside a funeral pyre where a body had just been cremated. The smell of smoldering wood and the acrid aroma of burned flesh was still strong in the summer night as he took handfuls of the charred wood from the pyre and crumbled it between his fingers, throwing out fragments of bone and flesh before rubbing the ash over his hair and body in the ascetic's bath that would increase the power of his meditations.

Crossing his legs in the lotus position, the Naga Baba placed his hands on his knees and began the chant he would continue for nine days and nine nights by that funeral pyre:

"Shiva-o-ham
I that am Shiva
Shiva-o-ham
Shiva am I."

Throughout that time people came and looked at the Naga Baba. But they only did so from a distance and in the bright light of day. Among them were a few who could tell from his saffron-covered trident that he belonged to one of the great Naga academies renowned for the wars they had fought to defend their faith. They warned their children not to disturb him, and in whispers told each other of the time during the Indian Mutiny when twenty thousand Naga ascetics, naked, ash-covered with matted locks, had come down from their caves in the Himalayas to do battle with the red-coated Englishmen ambitious for empire.

But at night, as the moon waned and then gave no light at all, no one had the courage to approach the cremation ground where for nine nights the Naga Baba sat chanting by the funeral pyre.

Then at last it was the night of Shiva.

On this night the Lord of Death became the death of death, and Shiva's acolytes broke their fasts by begging at the houses of those who were unclean, untouchable, or profane.

After smearing ash from the pyre onto his body, the Naga Baba went first to the house of the Dom. Every year the Naga Baba performed this ritual, and every year he heard the litany of cruelties endured by those society counted untouchable. Tonight was no different. The Dom complained bitterly about being an outcast as he poured water into the Naga Baba's bowl, but it did not prevent the ascetic from drinking two pitcherfuls of water to quench his thirst.

Wiping his mouth, the Naga Baba asked, "Can you direct me to where the lowest caste live?"

"Go past the mango plantations. You will find a sweeper colony on the outskirts of the town."

The Naga Baba set out for the colony, thinking about the people he had encountered in his long years as an ascetic.

At the academy he had learned the arts of a protector sadhu. He had been taught to wield his iron trident as a weapon. He had performed yogic contortions to gain a physical prowess far exceeding any wrestler's, hardened his hands and his feet so they could kill a man with a single blow, practiced mind control to disarm an opponent without touching him, and he was called a Naga.

But when he encountered the suffering of ordinary people, he did nothing to protect them beyond placing a tilak of ash on their foreheads before moving on in search of solitude.

The sweepers were waiting in front of their colony with offerings of food. They knew how much the ascetic honored them by eating from their hands. When he marked their foreheads with ash, they touched his feet in gratitude, denied such blessing from the temples that they were forbidden to enter.

Now the Naga Baba had to beg alms from a third unclean house before he could return to the jungle. "Is there a brothel in this town?"

"Of course, Baba."

"We will take you there."

The Naga Baba followed the sweepers through the narrow alleys behind their colony, observing how other people moved away from their approach and how the sweepers turned sideways to hide their faces, their whole stance one of shame. Angered by those who avoided his companions, the Naga Baba lifted his trident and roared, "om namo Shivaya! The name of God is Shiva, Lord of

Death!" Men and women ran into their doorways, terrified they might be cursed by the naked man shouting at them, his matted hair swinging from side to side.

The Naga Baba was pleased to see the sweepers still laughing behind their hands as they took him into a brightly lit bazaar and pointed to the wooden door of the brothel, outlined in a string of colored electric bulbs.

Film music blared from the brothel's balcony as the Naga Baba pounded the door with his trident. At last the door was flung open by a sweating man with a black thread tied around his throat for luck, muscles bulging under his cotton jerkin.

The Naga Baba proferred his skull bowl. "Alms. On the night of Shiva."

"Get away!" the man shouted. "We feed no beggars here!"

The Naga Baba raised his hand. "I am an ascetic of Shiva. Do you dare to turn me away tonight?"

The man fell back as if some magnetic force were pushing against his chest, although he had not been touched. A fat woman appeared at the man's shoulder, her face framed by golden earrings rendered gimcrack under the colored lights above the doorway. She opened betel-stained lips in surprise when she saw the ascetic.

"Jai Shankar! Praise to Shiva!"

The earrings slapped against her rouged cheeks as she bent to touch the Naga Baba's feet, and the ascetic looked into the brothel. A child was cowering behind a plastic-covered sofa, her face twisted with pain as a man gripped her chin in one hand. With his other hand the man was lifting the child's small body to bring her lips closer to his own.

The Naga Baba lost sight of the child as the woman stood up, saying "I have some lovely pistachio sweetmeats, specially bought for the night of Shiva."

"I have already eaten."

"But you must accept something. You cannot leave my house without blessing me."

"Then I will accept that child as alms tonight."

"Of course, Baba." The woman wrested the child from the arms of the irate customer and carried the unresisting form to the ascetic. The child stood before the Naga Baba, her head hardly higher than his knee, staring down at the ground. The woman hit the back of the child's head. It was not a gentle blow.

"Touch his feet with your forehead, you fool." The child groveled obediently at the ascetic's feet and the woman asked with a knowing smirk,

"Where shall I send my man to fetch her in the morning?"

"Do you give alms to the holy in expectation of having them returned?"

"But I paid five hundred rupees for her. It was a great charity I did her father. When I bought her there was no flesh on her at all. See how well I feed her, and still there is not enough of her to satisfy a man. Why not accept the sweets instead?"

The Naga Baba lifted his skull bowl to the woman's eyes, reversing it so she could put nothing in it.

"Then take her for the night, two nights even. If you still want to keep her so badly, come back in twelve or thirteen years. She won't be any good to me by then."

"If I leave your house empty-handed on the night of Shiva, if you refuse alms to the beloved of the Destroyer . . ."

"Take her!" The woman shrank back into the brothel, intimidated by the ascetic's eyes still red from the smoke of the funeral pyres, his body and his matted locks still gray with the ashes of the dead. "And do not curse me later when you find what trouble she brings. She doesn't even have a name. Her own father calls her misfortune."

The ascetic smeared ash on the woman's forehead before bending down to take the child's hand. The small fingers were rigid in his palm as she followed him from the open doorway of the brothel into the street.

When they were clear of the bazaar, the Naga Baba let go of the child's hand. He did not help her when they had to cross a street or climb over the low wall enclosing the town's small railway station. He merely shortened his steps and walked more slowly, intoning in his deep voice, "Om namo Shivaya, Om namo Shivaya," knowing the endless repetition of the chant "The name of God is Shiva, Shiva is God's name" would calm the child's fears as his teacher's voice had once mesmerized him into walking distances he had not imagined possible.

They passed the last lamp post of the town, and the dim lights from the sweepers' colony. Still the Naga Baba did not stop, although the night of India was closing over their heads and the howling of hyenas grew so close he knew they had entered the forest.

Now the Naga Baba took the child's hand again and helped her over the roots breaking through the dark earth of the jungle, until they reached a banyan tree so ancient its many branches had already plunged new roots into the ground.

The Naga Baba circled the tree collecting grass to make a bed for the child. She followed close behind, frightened by the dark and the rustling of night animals.

"How long have you lived in the brothel?" the Naga Baba asked as he spread the grass on the ground between the rooted branches of the banyan, patting the grass down to give it the firmness of a mattress.

"At least two rainy seasons."

"We shall spend the next rainy season in Amarkantak. Now sleep."

The Naga Baba sat near the child, his eyes closed in meditation, his deep chanting a steady drone that gentled her terror until she slept. He had already decided not to return to the jungle where he had been living earlier. It was too close to the town, too close to the brothel owner who might change her mind and send her bazaar toughs to take the child back.

The next morning he husked a fallen coconut and split it in half with a single blow to make a bowl for the child. Then they began walking north, toward the Narmada.

The journey took many weeks. On the way the child looked for water snakes, learning where they swam the water was pure enough to drink. She watched the ascetic dig bulbs and tubers from the ground to roast over an open fire, and was surprised at how good they tasted and how they filled her stomach.

He taught her to drink fresh milk directly from the teats of wandering goats, and how to look for cattle markings. Together they collected pats of cow dung to be left in the sun to dry. The Naga Baba made a small fire and burned the dung so it would crumble between his fingers into ash that he smeared all over his body, an antiseptic and an insulation against heat and cold. When he rubbed the mixture on her arms she found mosquitoes never bit her.

Their days were not lonely. Always there were people to be encountered, shepherds or villagers foraging for firewood, who shouted to the Naga Baba, "Jai Shankar! Praise to Shiva!"

Sometimes they brought food for the ascetic and his small companion. The child watched the Naga Baba separate the food into four equal portions—one to be kept aside for the animals, one for any stranger who might need a meal, saving only the remaining two portions for themselves.

As her new life became more real to her than her old, she told the Naga Baba about her father and three brothers who worked breaking stones by the roadside.

"I was never allowed to eat until everyone else

had eaten, so I was always hungry. And I was beaten by my father."

"Why did your father call you misfortune?"

"Because my mother died giving birth to me. Then this woman came to the slum where we lived, saying she needed young girls to work as servants for her clients. I believed my father when he told me God had given me a new mother. I was happy when he sold me to her. But that woman never treated me like a daughter. She just kept me in that house for those men."

"What is your real name?"

"I don't know. In that house they called me Chand, Moonlight."

"Why?"

"The customers chose the name, they said my skin is as soft as moonlight."

"When we reach our destination," the Naga Baba said gently, "you will never have to fear such men again."

And so they climbed the jagged hills of the Satpura Range until they reached the Amarkantak plateau.

Now they were in dense jungle crossed by tributaries or broken by sudden clearings in which there was a lake. The child saw wild elephants and white-faced monkeys. She learned to recognize herds of deer—blue bull, black buck, chinkara. She saw how animals came near the Naga Baba because he did not fear them, even the leopards she heard coughing at night, and when she fell asleep with the Naga Baba chanting next to her, deep in meditation, she knew the animals would ignore them as they ignored other species unthreatening to themselves.

As they neared the Narmada, villagers walked alongside to show them where the boatmen who piloted the ferries could be found. Each time they reached a tributary the Naga Baba assured the child they were closer to their destination. Trusting the ascetic, she suppressed her fear of men and waded into the water to be helped into some small country craft by a wiry boatman, his skin blackened from the sun, who counted it a blessing to carry a Naga ascetic in his boat.

Finally they reached the banks of the Narmada and the Naga Baba told the child she was nearly home.

"But we must cross to the other side of the river. Then no one will be able to find you. This great body of water divides India. Even the years and days are calculated differently on the other bank. You will begin a new life there. I will teach you to read and write. And I will give you a new name."

"What will you call me?"

"Uma."

"What does it mean?"

"It is another name for the goddess," the Naga Baba replied, lifting her into a large, flat-bottomed ferry crowded with farmers taking their produce to a weekly market. " 'Uma' means 'peace in the night.' "

On the boat the farmers queued for the Naga Baba's blessings. He smeared ash on their foreheads and they filled his bowl with coins and fruit as the child whispered her new name to herself. When they reached the other riverbank again the boatman took no money, and the child stood on the bank waving to the boatman until she could no longer see the boat at the turn of the river.

Still repeating her new name to herself, she followed the Naga Baba as he walked further and further upstream.

The Naga Baba did not stop until they reached a waterfall. "There is a cave behind that waterfall where we will live in the summer," he said, unwinding the saffron cloth that covered his iron trident. "But we must build a house to live in during the winter and the monsoons."

Now the child helped the Naga Baba collect large banana leaves to be plaited into a roof. She watched the ascetic cut down bamboo branches with his trident and drive the poles into the red earth of the riverbank. She stood on his shoulders to lay the plaited banana leaves across the poles, laughing with delight when he lowered her to the ground and she saw they had built a two-room hut.

"There remains one last ceremony."

The Naga Baba gave the child a pat of dried cow dung and led her through the lengthening shadows cast by the trees toward the river. "Do you know which night I found you?"

"When?" the child asked, uncertain if the wriggling shadow at her feet was a moving vine or a snake.

"The night of Shiva, Lord of Death. Your other life died that night. See this stick of sandalwood? I will grind it into ash and put it on your forehead when you meet your new mother."

The child threw the cow dung on the ground and started running, thrashing through the plants in her desperation to get away from the ascetic.

Her father had told her she was going to a new mother when he sold her to the brothel. She knew the Naga Baba had sold her again.

The Naga Baba grabbed her, his breathing harsh above the stems breaking under his feet as he carried her through the darkness toward the river. Placing her on the wet mud of the river-bank, he reached up to wind his matted locks on top of his head. Suddenly he gripped her arms and lowered her into the water. "The Narmada claims all girls as hers. Tonight you become a daughter of the Narmada."

The paralyzed child stared into the ascetic's eyes. The ash from his hair was falling onto her face, the cold current soaked her rigid body. Then the water closed over the child's head and she heard only the sound of her own blood pounding in her ears. She no longer even had the will to scream, knowing she could do nothing to prevent herself from being drowned, helpless in the grip of the Naga Baba's powerful hands.

But the Naga Baba was already lifting her out of the river. Ignoring the child's tears, he began to burn his stick of sandalwood so that it gave off a musky sweet smell in the jungle. He crumbled the sandalwood between his fingers until it dis-integrated, then drew three streaks of ash across the child's forehead.

"There," he said with satisfaction. "Now we can go home."

He led the child past the ancient trees that lined the riverbank, holding the jasmine and lantana creepers to one side so she could precede him down the path. Together they circled the tumbling shadows of a giant bamboo thicket and clambered down the rocks leading to the waterfall.

As they entered the cave beneath the plunging river the ascetic sang,

"Turtles and river dolphins find refuge in your waters
Alighting herons play upon your tranquil surface.
Fish and crocodiles are gathered in your embrace.
O holy Narmada."

That summer the child and the Naga Baba lived in the cave behind the waterfalls. The ascetic taught the child to read and write, and at night he sang to her of the Narmada. Over the months the child heard the songs so often she asked to learn them herself.

Only when she had fallen asleep did the Naga Baba begin his own meditations, so that sometimes in her dreams she heard his deep voice chanting

"Shiva-o-ham
I that am Shiva
Shiva-o-ham
Shiva am I."

When the season of rains came, the Naga Baba and the child moved from the cave into the hut they had built on the riverbank from plaited banana leaves and bamboo poles.

Often the monsoons storms were so heavy the swollen waters of the river flooded their banks, swirling around the tree trunks and the bamboo thickets until they flowed right into the hut, as if trying to embrace the child learning to recite the river's praises.

CHAPTER SIXTEEN

THE SONG OF THE NARMADA

"Is that when you met the Naga Baba?" I asked.

A group of scholars peered into the veranda and Tariq Mia sighed, waving them in the direction of the mosque. "It must be late, little brother. I have to join my students."

He tried to stand up but his legs wouldn't support him, stiff from sitting too long.

"Is that when you met them?" I repeated, helping him to his feet.

"Yes, they lived on this riverbank for nearly three years. Each time I saw Uma she knew more songs about the river. When she grew older the Naga Baba encouraged her to sing at temple festivals, so they were always traveling from temple to temple."

The old mullah released my hands and

stretched his limbs gingerly. "She told me she was being called a singer-saint when I last met her. But that time she came alone. The Naga Baba had left her to follow the next stage of his enlightenment."

We walked slowly to the bridge, his fingers resting on my arm with a pressure so light it was as if he had already discarded his frail body.

As we crossed the marble platform in front of the mosque, Tariq Mia remarked, "I didn't think the Naga Baba would ever leave Uma. She was more than a child to him. She was the fruit of his austerity."

I asked what he meant. Tariq Mia paused at the bridge, staring into the water, his narrow face thrown into shadow by the flame tree above his head spraying its bright feathers of red and orange petals against the green fruit of a nearby banana tree.

"Maybe it's only an old man's foolishness, little brother. But if the Narmada was born from Shiva's penance, then surely Uma was born of the Naga Baba's penance. Tell me, what higher enlightenment could he acquire by leaving her?"

"Shall I try and find them for you? No one is staying at the bungalow. I have plenty of free time."

The old mullah's thin arms embraced me.

"Such people are like water flowing water through our lives, little brother. We learn something from the encounter, then they are gone. We never find them again."

I stood on the bridge watching Tariq Mia walk toward the mosque where his students were waiting for him. He did not turn to wave good-bye. His eyes were fixed on the marble platform beneath his feet.

The smell of vegetation rose from the earth as I followed the mud path through the trees back to the bungalow.

The jungle was seething with activity. Parakeets and cuckoos, wood pigeons and mynahs shrieked and cawed as they built their nests before the heat of summer seared the forest. Even deer and wild boar were crossing the path undisturbed by any tribal women collecting firewood.

I was wondering where the women were this morning when I heard shouting and the sound of engines coming from the direction of the bungalow. I sprinted down the mud path, fearing an accident.

As I reached the bend I saw a group of Vano village women unloading crates from three jeeps parked in a line outside the rest house.

Mr. Chagla was standing by the jeeps, ticking

off items on an inventory. Behind him Dr. Mitra was waving his lanky arms at a tall man following two girls dressed in trousers into the bungalow grounds.

"Ah, there you are!" Dr. Mitra shouted when he saw me. "Shankar, Shankar, hang on. I want you to meet your host."

The man turned. His cropped hair was almost military in its exactness, his spare frame marred only by a protruding belly, its roundness more befitting a trader than someone Dr. Mitra was introducing as Professor V. V. Shankar, the foremost archaeological authority on the Narmada in the country.

"Forgive the suddenness of our arrival," Professor Shankar said in a deep voice, shaking my hand. "We are conducting an archaeological dig forty kilometers from here. Dr. Mitra suggested I live here and use your rest house as our headquarters."

He nodded at the two girls behind him. "These are my assistants, Sheela and Asha. They will be living at the camp."

A man with a mustache leaned over the balcony above us. Another man, his cherubic features suggesting he was hardly out of his teens, shouted over the first man's shoulder, "We've finally got the field telephone working, Professor! Old Murli wants a word with you. Some peasant's got his cattle wandering all over the site."

"I'll be right up, Naresh. You, Anil, start organizing the library." Professor Shankar pushed past the girls and ran down the garden, calling back to us, "It must be an emergency if my old guide Murli wants my advice."

I watched the activity around me in astonishment. Mr. Chagla was urging the village women into the bungalow. As they trooped past me I read the stenciled markings on the wooden crates balanced on their heads: Microscopes, Chemicals, Research Slides, Photographic Equipment, Reference Books. Behind us the two girls were dragging more crates from the jeeps.

Dr. Mitra laughed at my dazed expression. "Oh, come on, it's not going to be as bad as all that. You're only going to have Shankar staying here. He's a good chap. We're old friends, you know. The rest of them will be forty kilometers away. Come on, let's get out of here before we are run over."

He took my elbow between his bony fingers and led me through the crowded garden into the drawing room as if he were leading a patient with a migraine into a darkened chamber.

"But who is this Professor Shankar?" I demanded as the archaeologist's deep voice shouting into his field telephone echoed down the stairs. "Does he work for the government?"

"Not now. He used to head the Archaeological Department for this whole part of the country until he got so fed up with red tape he resigned from government service."

Dr. Mitra unfolded his long frame into an armchair. "After Shankar resigned no one heard from him for absolute ages. Then three years ago he resurfaced with a remarkable book, *The Narmada Survey.* Apparently he had been researching it all that time. Anyway the book made a huge splash in archaeological circles, and he was invited to become chairman of the Indian Preservation Trust. The trust is financing this dig."

The door opened. One of Professor Shankar's assistants entered, breezily brushing her thick short hair away from her eyes. "Sorry for the interruption. Could you organize a quick lunch? We promised our guide we would set up camp before nightfall."

I shrugged helplessly at Dr. Mitra, who rolled his eyes in sympathy as I went to look for Mr. Chagla.

By the time we filed into the dining room I could see the cook and Mr. Chagla had been inspired by the unexpected challenge to produce an enormous meal.

The expedition members pulled their chairs up to the table and helped themselves unselfconsciously from the dishes spread before them, craning past the bearers coming in with hot breads and rice to argue with each other about the dig.

There was an energy at the table that brought back memories of my own days as a government officer when we were working to meet the deadline for the next budget.

"Will we get a book as good as *The Narmada Survey* out of this dig, Professor?" the assistant with the mustache asked. Without waiting for a reply he announced, "Professor Shankar worships the Narmada, you know. That's why he's such an expert on it."

"Rubbish," Professor Shankar admonished him. "I love this river. But worship is too strong a word."

"Why?" Dr. Mitra argued. "After all, the Narmada is the holiest river in India, as our host would be the first to tell us."

Professor Shankar glanced up and I was conscious of being assessed by the fierce intelligence in the black eyes behind the thick spectacles.

"I'm afraid I only care for the river's immortality, not its holiness," he said dryly.

"What do you mean by immortality?" I asked, embarrassed that everyone was looking at me.

Professor Shankar took off his heavy spectacles and wiped them carefully with a handkerchief, revealing indentations on either side of his nose. "Well, the Narmada is what we call a degrading river. It has a very fast current, which erodes the riverbed, cutting deeper and deeper into the rock. But the Narmada has never changed its course. What we are seeing today is the same river that was seen by the people who lived here a hundred thousand years ago. To me such a sustained record of human presence in the same place—that is immortality."

Dr. Mitra shook his head. "Unchangeability perhaps, but surely not immortality?"

"No, no. Mitra. I mean immortality in its most literal sense. So much so, the Hindu calendar is different on either bank of the Narmada. Just think. Thousands of years ago the sage Vyasa dictated the *Mahabharata* on this riverbank. Then in our own century this region provided the setting for Kipling's *Jungle Book*. In between countless other men have left their mark on the river."

An assistant grimaced at her fellow scholars. "For instance, Kalidasa. His poem *The Cloud Messenger* and his great play *Shakuntala* both describe the hills behind this rest house."

I could see the conversation was a familiar game to the professor's assistants as the other girl said, "Then twelve hundred years ago Shankara-charya composed a poem to the river."

"What about all the poems Rupmati and Baz Bahadur wrote when the Narmada appeared to them as a spring from under a tamarind tree not so far from here?" asked one of the men.

Professor Shankar laughed and pushed his chair back. "Precisely. Providing archaeologists with too much work to be wasting time like this."

He took a handkerchief out of his pocket. Wiping the perspiration from his closely cropped hair, he led Dr. Mitra and his assistants from the dining room. A moment later the drivers gunned their engines. With a roar of acceleration the convoy bounced down the mud road toward the archaeo-logical site.

An oppressive silence descended on the rest house when they were gone, and an air of being left behind seemed to infuse the dining room. Even the bearers were moving lethargically as they cleared the table.

Mr. Chagla gave me a dejected glance. "They brought so much life, no, sir? So much life, so much—"

"Better get in some supplies, Chagla," I interrupted impatiently. "You saw how much they ate."

· · ·

Within a week the routine of the rest house was dominated by the archaeologists. They now occupied the entire first floor of the bungalow. Professor Shankar lived in one suite. The others had been turned into a laboratory, a library, and a communications room containing the field telephone and charts.

Every morning Mr. Chagla personally supervised the cleaning of the rooms, worried that an overconscientious servant might sweep away a fragment of the distant past, thinking it to be only a broken piece of stone or a clod of mud.

I no longer visited Tariq Mia's village, in case my services should suddenly be required at the rest house. Even so, I usually found the professor gone to the site before I returned from my morning walk. But one or more of his assistants would arrive during the morning and disappear into the laboratory, where they would work all day. Or they would shout into the field telephone asking Professor Shankar for instructions, their voices loud through the open windows above the garden. At lunchtime their high spirits and keen appetites filled the dining room with boisterous energy.

Then at five o'clock the bungalow emptied as the assistants left for their camp. Mr. Chagla made a last inspection of the suites before mounting his bicycle to return to Rudra, and I was left to enjoy the tranquility of the deserted rest house for a few hours until Professor Shankar came back from the site and joined me on the terrace in the evenings.

Sometimes we sat together in silence watching the distant silhouettes of the pilgrims floating their lamps on the water at Mahadeo, moving like ants up and down the temple steps.

Sometimes, sipping at a glass of watermelon juice, Professor Shankar would talk about the river.

Once I asked him why he did not think the river was sacred. His reply was so derisive I never repeated the question.

"Mere mythology! A waste of time! If anything is sacred about this river, it is the individual experiences of the human beings who have lived here."

Professor Shankar pointed into the darkness. "Look to your left. Where the waterfalls are. When I was researching my book I discovered some cave drawings in that area. Our datings of the rock samples prove they are from the Stone Age. So they must be among the oldest evidence of human life in India. Lower down the same cliff we are finding implements from successive ages— Neolithic, Iron, Bronze."

He picked up his glass and drained it. "This river is an unbroken record of the human race. That is why I am here. Now tell me why you are here."

I knew my answer would sound foolish, but I still said, "I have retired from the world."

"What were you doing before you retired?"

"I was a bureaucrat. Quite senior, as a matter of fact."

He waited for me to continue but I could not bring myself to tell him of the privileges of my previous life: the army of waiting clerks, the specially reserved train compartments, the supplicants. Or how often I had seen my colleagues succumb to corruption and how, each time, my urge to leave the world had grown stronger.

"You have chosen the wrong place to flee the world, my friend," Professor Shankar said at last, getting up to leave the terrace. "Too many lives converge on these banks."

I nodded agreement although the archaeologist was already moving across the dark lawn toward the lights of the veranda. I was thinking of the people I had encountered since I had come to the rest house, and Tariq Mia's observation that they were like water flowing through lives to teach us something. Perhaps the old mullah was right. Perhaps destiny had brought me to the banks of the

Narmada to understand the world. Suddenly, for the first time since the archaeologists had arrived, I recalled Tariq Mia's tale about the Naga Baba and his charge.

"Professor Shankar!" I called after the archaeologist. He turned expectantly. "I still know so little about the river. If you meet any river minstrels, could you send them to me?"

He took out his handkerchief and rubbed his head, the sound of cloth on his short hair distinct in the night. "I suppose I could ask my old guide to look out for them."

"Wouldn't you enjoy listening to a Narmada minstrel?"

He waved dismissively at me from the bungalow veranda. "Not I, my friend. Minstrels sing about gods and goddesses. I am a man, and only understand songs about other men. The rest I leave to you."

He took off his spectacles and looked at his watch. "By the way, tomorrow I am taking my assistants to a site farther up river. We'll set up camp at the dig itself, so count on us being gone for a week. I expect you'll enjoy having a little peace again."

To my surprise Professor Shankar's prediction proved wrong. I had also thought I would enjoy my solitude when the archaeologists were gone, despite my pleasure at the presence of the trousered girls, or the two young men always smoking cigarettes, whose activity enlivened the bungalow with the restless energy of the city.

I even gave Mr. Chagla the week off.

I had not suspected that I would feel so lonely while they were away. I found I missed the noisy lunches with the young archaeologists and their infectious enthusiasm when describing the progress of their excavations. I found I missed Professor Shankar and the pleasure of talking to a companion who shared my own background of government service.

Sitting on the terrace, meditating in the darkness before dawn, I admitted to myself that I envied the archaeologists for still belonging to a world that I had given up.

Now that I had the leisure I no longer had the inclination to visit Tariq Mia. I did not want to sit with the mullah of a small village that seemed frozen in time, untouched by the events of a larger world. With some alarm I realized I was becoming accustomed to that other rhythm the archaeologists had brought into the rest house, the rhythm of my previous life.

Without their presence the days stretched aimlessly before me, and the small tasks that occupied me in the running of the bungalow did not make the time pass more quickly.

I was relieved when the week drew to an end and I could anticipate welcoming Professor Shankar and his assistants back to the empty bungalow.

The evening before the archaeologists were to return I was sitting by myself on the veranda of the rest house, able to enjoy again the river breeze in that half hour before the sun sets, when the guard coughed below the veranda to attract my attention.

"There is a woman at the gate who wants to see you, sahib."

"What does she want?"

"I don't know, sahib. She says she must speak to you."

"I suppose you'd better fetch her."

A moment later the guard returned, followed by a slender young woman dressed in a crimson sari, holding a one-stringed instrument on her left shoulder. As she approached I saw the silver finger cymbals tied to her right hand.

"I believe you wish to hear a recitation of the river, sahib. I am a river minstrel."

I asked her name and who had sent her to the

bungalow. She said nothing, not even nodding her head in answer to my questions. Oddly, her reticence did not offend me. Trying to disguise my excitement, I led her to the terrace.

Beyond the terrace the sun was striking the canals on the opposite riverbank. They glittered silver in the green fields as the minstrel laid her instrument on the stone floor and walked to the parapet.

Folding her hands, she chanted to the water,

"The sages have said
Whoever praises you
At dawn, at dusk, at night
May in this human form
Acquired through the suffering of
So many rebirths
Approach with honor
The feet of Shiva Himself.

"Then hear my praise,
O holy Narmada.

"You grace the earth
With your presence.
The devout call you Kripa
Grace itself.

"You cleanse the earth
Of its impurities.
The devout call you Surasa
The holy soul.

"You leap through the earth
Like a dancing deer.
The devout call you Rewa
The leaping one.

"But Shiva called you
Delight
And laughing
Named you Narmada."

She gestured to me to sit down and picked up
her instrument. The clash of finger cymbals produced a gentle beat under the drone of her instrument.

"O copper-colored water
Below a copper-colored sky
From Shiva's penance you became water.
From water you became a woman
So beautiful that gods and ascetics
Their loins hard with desire

Abandoned their contemplations
To pursue you.

"Once and only once
In the turning Wheel of Existence
The Terrible One was moved to laughter.
Looking from his inward contemplation
To watch you The Destroyer said,
  O damsel of the beautiful hips,
  Evoker of Narma, lust,
  Be known as Narmada
  Holiest of rivers."

Above us the sky was turning metallic. The soft
light bronzed the minstrel's features as she sang.

"O river, born of penance
Named by laughter,
Your disheveled streams
Inlay the stone mountains of the Vindhyas
Like ichor gilds the body of an elephant.
And along your riverbanks
The stamens of the green gold Nipa
  flowers
Tear through their enclosing petals
Desiring you.

"Woodlands heavy with wild jasmine
Embrace you with their fragrance.
Hearing your approach
Young plantain trees
Burst into sudden blossom."

The sun was setting and a torrent of colors flooded the sky, playing across the minstrel's features.

"The sages meditating on your riverbanks say
You are twice-born,
Once from penance,
Once from love.

"They say the Ascetic sporting with the
    goddess
Mingled the sweat of his ardor with the
    drops
Of love's exertions from her breasts
Creating you from the liquid of his divine
    desire.

"Then he changed you into a river
To cool the lusts of holy men
And called you Narmada,
Soother of Desires.

"Even Shiva's semen
Is cooled to stone in your riverbed
Each seed becoming
An idol wrested from your blue-black
    waters,
Worshipped with flower garlands
In the temples on your banks."

The minstrel closed her eyes and seemed to
enter a trance, as she swayed from side to side.

"O river born of love,
Named by laughter,
Your purple waters slip like a garment
From your sloping banks.

"Kalidasa asks who can bear to leave you?
For who can bear to leave a woman, her
    loins bared,
Having once seen the sweetness of her body?

"Leaping antelopes
Chart your course.
Birds throng the sacred trees
Shading your village squares.
Rose apples darken your water.

Wild mangoes fall into your coiling current
Like flowers in a maiden's hair."

The sun had disappeared into the horizon. In the twilight the swaying minstrel's face was indistinct.

"It is written in the scriptures
That you were present at the birth of time
When Shiva as a golden peacock
Roamed the ocean of the Void.

"You reminded the Destroyer
Creation awaited His command.
Fanning then his terrible feathers,
Shiva brought forth this world and the
mountain
Where he sits in meditation
Until the Destruction.

"You were present at the Creation
By Shiva's command you alone will remain
At the Destruction."

She turned to face me and she no longer seemed young. Perhaps it was the unlit bungalow rising like the shadow of a deserted temple behind her that made her now seem ageless.

"It is foretold by the wise who know the truth,
At midnight when the dark flood comes
You will turn into a girl
As radiant as a column of luster.

"Holding a trident in your slender hand you
will say
'Sages, leave your forest hermitages.
Do not delay. The time of great destruction
is here.

" 'While the Destroyer dances
All will be destroyed.
I and I alone am sanctuary.

" 'Bring your knowledge of mankind
And follow me.
I will lead you to the next Creation.' "

A figure was crossing the garden. As he came nearer I saw it was Professor Shankar. The minstrel did not see him. She was swaying with her instrument, facing the river to sing Shankaracharya's hymn,

"O Messenger of Passing Time,
O Sanctuary and Salvation,

You dissolve the fear of time itself.
O holy Narmada.

"You remove the stains of evil.
You release the wheel of suffering.
You lift the burdens of the world.
O holy Narmada."

Professor Shankar stepped onto the terrace and a smile brightened the minstrel's face.

"Turtles and river dolphins find refuge in your
*   waters*
Alighting herons play upon your tranquil
*   surface.*
Fish and crocodiles are gathered in your
*   embrace.*
O holy Narmada.

"Bards and ascetics sing your wonders.
Gamblers, cheats, and dancers praise you.
We all find refuge in your embrace
O holy Narmada."

The minstrel folded her hands to the river. For a moment she stood with her head bowed above the dark water. Then, laying her instrument on the floor, she walked toward us.

I reached into my pocket for money but she moved past me and bent to touch Professor Shankar's feet.

Professor Shankar raised her from the ground. "Are you well, Uma?"

"Yes, Naga Baba. They said you wanted me to come."

I stared at the two of them in shock, unable to comprehend what was happening.

"Where do you go from here?"

"I am making my way to the coast."

Professor Shankar laughed. "To find a husband, like the Narmada found her Lord of Rivers?"

"You can see into the future, Naga Baba. You know if it will be so."

"The future reveals itself to everyone in time. Come, I'll drive you back to Rudra."

He moved forward to help the minstrel with her instrument. I stepped between them.

"You?" I demanded. "An ascetic?"

"Not any more."

"But you can't be the Naga Baba!"

I waited for him to contradict me. He remained silent, watching me through his heavy spectacles.

"You can't be the Naga Baba!" I shouted, frustrated by the archaeologist's silence. "He is in a cave somewhere, seeking higher enlightenment."

"No. He has reentered the world."

I gripped Professor Shankar's arm. He did not move but I felt I was being pushed backward and my fingers lost their hold.

Professor Shankar observed my agitation with polite indifference as I struggled to form another question.

"What do you want to know?" he asked at last.

"Why you became an ascetic, why you stopped. What all this means."

"I have no great truths to share, my friend," he said patiently. "I told you, I am only a man."

I could not believe my ears. "Was it worth so much pain to discover something so obvious?"

Professor Shankar remained silent, and again his silence infuriated me.

"Is this your enlightenment? Is this why you endured all those penances?"

He gave me an ironic smile. "Don't you know the soul must travel through eighty-four thousand births in order to become a man?"

He turned and I almost didn't hear him add, "Only then can it reenter the world."

I tried to decipher the meaning of his words as Professor Shankar walked toward the minstrel waiting at the end of the terrace.

He put his arm around the minstrel's slender shoulder. They moved across the garden toward the gate. I stood there in the darkness watching them, unable to believe he had ever been a naked ascetic, unable to convince myself he had not.

The jeep doors slammed shut and headlights pierced the jungle, throwing strange shadows across the bamboo groves. Sudden arcs of light raked the darkness as the jeep roared down the twisting path that led to Rudra. I stared at the flashes of illumination, wondering for the first time what I would do if I ever left the bungalow.

The jeep disappeared around the curve of the hill into the night and I turned back to the terrace.

The temple bells were clanging in the distance at Mahadeo. Behind me the servants were switching on the lights in the bungalow.

I leaned over the parapet to look at the river.

Below the terrace the water flowed black under a moonless sky.

At the bend of the river the clay lamps were still flickering as the current carried them toward the ocean.

GLOSSARY

Ahimsa Nonviolence.

Almirah Cupboard.

Ashes Mark of the ascetic. The ash bath is supposed to convey spiritual powers; in mythology Shiva took the first ash bath in the ashes of the God of Love, Kama, whom Shiva had incinerated for disturbing his meditations.

Benares Also Varanasi, Kasi. One of the seven sacred cities of the Hindus, situated on the Ganges River.

Betel Vine. Its leaves and juice are used as a digestive.

Bidi Cheroot made from a rolled tobacco leaf.

Boddhistava Enlightened being, teacher of truth.

Brahmin Member of the priestly caste, a scholar class.

Chandidas (c. 1350–1430) Bengali poet whose songs dealt with every form of human love and inspired the great Hindu reformer, Chaitanya.

Chisti Thirteenth-century Sufi mystic who settled in the city of Ajmer and introduced his mystic order to India. Considered one of the four founder saints of Indo-Sufism. Died in Ajmer.

Collyrium Medicated lampblack, used as an eyeliner.

Dhoti A single-piece garment of cloth worn by men; hangs in folds from the waist to the ankles.

Diksha Literally, initiation.

Gandharva Veda The science of music, song, drama, dance. An appendage of the Sama Veda.

Great Moghul The emperor Akbar (1542–1605) who reigned from 1556 to 1605.

Harmonium Rectangular box with two bellows and a keyboard. It was thought to have been brought to India by the Portuguese in the seventeenth century as a pedal instrument, but is now a hand instrument played by the musician sitting cross-legged on the floor facing the keyboard.

Haveli Mansion constructed around interlocking courtyards; also used in northern India as a term for atelier.

Jain Indian religion of extreme antiquity. Its last reformer, Mahavira, (500 B.C.) is generally regarded as the historical founder of modern Jainism. In the first century A.D. the Jains split into two main sects—the Svetambara or white-clad group that wears white garments, and the Digambar or sky-clad group whose austerities ban the possession of clothing.

Jehangir (1569–1627) Son of Akbar and Moghul emperor from 1605 to 1627.

Kaaba In Mecca, a large black stone, now thought to be a meteorite, where the Prophet Muhammad broke the idols of the unbelievers and prayed.

Kabir (1440–1518) Reformer of the two great religions of India in his time, Hinduism and Islam. He scorned the rituals of both religions, the idolatry of the Hindus and the theological hair-splitting of the Muslims, and consigned the priests of both religions to hell. He also objected to the Jain and Buddhist emphasis on absolute abstinence from violence on the grounds that life sustained itself by preying on life. The founder of the Sikh religion was profoundly influenced by Kabir's insistence on truth, mercy, and self-control. Banned from the Hindu holy city of Benares, persecuted by the Muslim emperor Sikandar Lodi, Kabir was vastly popular with the masses and persecuted by the ruling classes.

Kailash The paradise of Shiva. A Himalayan mountain, north of Lake Manasa.

Kalidasa India's greatest poet and dramatist, one of the nine gems of King Vikramaditya's court at Ujjain. As there were several kings with that name at Ujjain, Kalidasa's work has been dated variously from 400 B.C. to A.D. 200.

Of his play *Shakuntala*, Goethe wrote,

Willst du den Himmel, die Erde, mit einem namen
*   begriefen*
Nenn' ich Sakuntala dich, und so ist alles gesagt.
*   (Can the earth and heaven itself in one name*
*   be combined?*
*   I name you, O Shakuntala, and all is said.)*

Kama God of love, incinerated by a glance from Shiva's third eye when he disturbed the meditating god. He then became known as Ananga, the bodiless one.

Kamarupa Ancient name for the current Indian region of Assam, an area associated with erotic cults of great antiquity. It is called the land of Kama because here Kama, God of Love, is thought to have regained his rupa, or physical form.

Kama Sutra An encyclopedia of erotic education, covering most aspects and techniques of courtship and sexual union, written by Vatsayana in the fifth century A.D.

Khusrau, Amir The first and greatest disciple of Nizamuddin Auliya, one of the founders of Indian Sufism. A poet and musician, he is credited with the invention of the modern sitar and the Urdu language. He died in Delhi, 1325.

Lingam Phallus of Shiva, symbolizing regenerative religion. Also elliptical stones polished by the action of the Narmada River, worshipped as the image of Shiva.

Mahabharata Epic poem of the Hindus, probably the longest poem in the world. It is said to have been dictated by the sage Vyasa. Its main theme is the war between the Kauravas and the Pandavas; in it the divine charioteer, Lord Krishna, expounds to King

Arjuna the philosophy that has become one of the central texts of the Hindus, the *Bhagavad Gita*, or the *Song of the Divine One.*

Mahout Elephant trainer.

Mecca Birthplace of the Prophet Muhammad; holiest city of Islam.

Mirabai (c. 1450–1520) Hindu poet and mystic. A Rajput queen who left her husband to worship her deity, Lord Krishna, Mirabai's songs to Krishna are sung all over India.

Mullah Religious teacher, in Islamic faith.

Naga Sadhus Naked ascetics, followers of Shiva. Also known as the protector ascetics.

Nawab Title for a Muslim ruler.

Nizamuddin Quarter in the capital of modern India, New Delhi. It contains the shrine of Nizamuddin Auliya, one of the founders of Indian Sufism, and also the tomb of Amir Khusrau, his most famous disciple. It has been the center of Quawwal music (songs in praise of God) since the thirteenth century A.D.

Paan Digestive made from betel leaf, lime paste, and crushed areca nut.

Paanwallah Vendor of paans.

Patiala peg Triple shot of whisky named after the Maharajah of Patiala, who was famous for his height and his appetites.

Pi-dog Mongrel.

Pukka Slang for "the real thing."

Purana Literally, ancient. Collection of texts giving legendary accounts of ancient times. Though the Puranas contain much earlier material handed down orally, their written dates are comparatively late—from the first century B.C. to the sixth century A.D. There are eighteen great Puranas and eighty-eight subordinate works also called puranas but not thought to have much merit.

Quawwali Singer of quawwals (literally, aphorisms), songs in praise of God. Quawwal music spread in India in the thirteenth century A.D. and was used by Sufi singer-saints to popularize their message. It is usually sung by a group of singers in a constant interchange of solo and choral modalities.

Raga Literally, shade or tint. Each raga, or modal melody, is supposed to color the mind of the listener with a specific emotion or musical atmosphere. These melodies constitute the highest expression of Indian classical music.

Raga-vivodha Composed in 1609 by Somanatha, this important musical text makes special reference to melodies in Indian classical music.

Rasa Literally, juice. An emotional state, in music the soul of the performance. The most ancient treatise on Indian art, *The Natya Shastra*—also sometimes called the Fifth Veda—defines rasa as the permanent mood experienced by the audience that can be conveyed only by a musician who has himself experienced the rasa. *The Natya Sastra* identifies eight rasas, each of which has a color and a presiding deity: Love, Laughter, Rage, Pathos, Terror, Disgust, Heroism, and Wonder. After the advent of Buddhism, a ninth rasa was added, Tranquility.

Rupee Indian currency, made up of 100 paisas.

Sadhu Holy man, ascetic.

Sari Garment worn by Indian women. A single piece of fabric six meters long is folded at the waist to fall to the ground, with one end draped over the shoulder.

Samosa Savory pastry filled with minced meat or vegetables.

Shankaracharya (c. 770–810) Religious teacher and reformer, believed by many in his lifetime to have been an incarnation of Shiva.

Shiva One of the three gods of the Hindu triad—Brahma, Vishnu, and Shiva. He is the supreme god to his votaries. Shiva is also thought to date from the pre-Hindu period. When worshipped as the God of Death, he is the oldest god in India.

Sufis Islamic mystics, a sect of the Shia Muslims. Indo-Sufism is based on the concept of mystical love with two central tenets: striving to unite with God by following the Way under the direction of a spiritual guide and ecstatic intuition of divinity through God's illumination. Indo-Sufism spread through the subcontinent in the thirteenth century A.D. The concept of the guide or teacher is very strong in Indo-Sufism, leading to veneration of Sufi saints and celebrations on their death anniversaries at their shrines to commemorate their final union with God. Sufis believe mystical love must be cultivated spiritually and aroused emotionally, leading to the great impact of the Quawwali singers in

India as a means of achieving the ecstasy in which God is found.

Sutra Literally, a thread or string. Also a term for literary forms, usually aphoristic in nature.

Tabla Pair of drums. The treble drum is played with the right hand and the bass drum is played with the left hand.

Tanpura A long gourd with four strings, used to provide a drone in support of main instrument or voice.

Tansen (1550–1610) One of India's greatest musicians and singers, considered one of the nine jewels of Emperor Akbar's court. A tamarind tree grows by his grave, and it is believed that singers who chew the leaves from this tree will acquire greater richness and purity of voice.

Tapas Ascetic heat or ardor; a kind of psychic explosion that leads in the case of the gods to the creation of universes, and with humans to the acquisition of such powers that even the gods tremble before them. Shiva as the supreme Ascetic sustains the universe through his tapas.

Tram Trolley car.

Tulsidas (c. 1527–1620) Poet and religious reformer who was abandoned by his parents and brought up by a wandering ascetic. He is also thought to have been influenced by the ideas of the Nestorian Christians.

Upanishads About 150 treatises of esoteric doctrines, generally thought to have been recorded in the sixth century B.C. With their remarkable freedom of exploration, they are considered to be the origins of Hindu metaphysical inquiry.

Vanaprasthi Forest hermit or forest dweller.

Vatsayana (fifth century A.D.) Greatest Indian authority on erotics. He is thought to have been himself an ascetic and a celibate.

Veda Divine knowledge of the Hindus in hymn form. They are thought to have been written from 2500 B.C. to 1000 B.C. There are four vedas—Rig, Yajur, Sama, and Atharva. The Rig Veda is the most ancient.

Veena India's most ancient stringed instrument. It is made of a wide wooden fingerboard with two gourds under the stem at each end, twenty-four frets, and six strings—four playing strings and two drone strings.

Viceroy Representative of the King of England, who was also Emperor of India, to India; head of the government of British India.

Vyasa Literally, arranger of the Vedas. Semilegendary sage of great antiquity, considered the author of the *Mahabharata.* He is supposed to have been the grandsire of the two royal lines who are the protagonists of the war described in the *Mahabharata.*

Yaar Slang for friend, pal.

Yoga One of the six schools of orthodox Hindu philosophy. It is also a form of mental and physical discipline codified by Patanjali in his Yoga Sutras. Additionally, it is a code of ascetic practices, mainly pre-Aryan in origin. It is the main expression of Indian meditation.

ACKNOWLEDGMENTS

My thanks to Sonny and John for the supply of notebooks; to Martand, for discussions about the Narmada; to Naveen, for his advice on the final story; to Princess Sita, for her Sanskrit translations; to Mr. Jain, of Manoharlal Munshiram Publishers of New Delhi, for locating research texts; to Dr. B. K. Thapar, for sharing his knowledge of the Narmada's archaeology; to Sonny and Aditya, for their observations on the manuscript; and finally, to the French scholar of Sanskrit browsing in a Delhi bookshop who introduced me to Shankaracharya's Invocation to the Narmada.

ABOUT THE AUTHOR

GITA MEHTA is the author of two previous books, *Karma Cola* and *Raj*. She has written, produced, and directed a number of documentaries for American, British, and European television companies and had articles published in several magazines. She is married, with one son, and divides her time among the United States, England, and India.